MW01126511

Autism
Over the Years

A Twelve Year Old's Memoir

By Micaela Ellis

ISBN-10: 0692194924

ISBN-13: 978-0692194928

Illustrations by Micaela Ellis

Cover design by Alex Mooney, Mooney Creative

Cover photography by Holly Roberts, Kadaya Photography

This book is dedicated to Mom for helping me develop my self-awareness over the years.

Contents

INTRODUCTION
by Gloria Ellis

As most parents do, I believe that my own child is absolutely amazing. But, I also happen to have some evidence of this personal truth. Some of that evidence is probably here in her book, and other pieces can be found only in my own memories and experiences raising her. Whether she is truly the greatest person alive or just a run-of-the-mill awesome kid, I hope that the following pages introduce whoever reads them to a few of her amazing qualities, which include her sense of humor, her self-awareness, her desire to know her place in the world, her love for her family and friends, and her kindness. Above all, I hope that, through her own words, her genuine wish for people to understand her (and others who, like her, are often misunderstood) is accomplished.

Micaela Ellis was born in 2005 to two first-time parents who had no idea what they were getting into. We were fairly young, both in school, and far from family or close friends. Micaela's first year of life was pretty standard, as far as we could tell, and our worries were similar to those of most other parents. Is she healthy? Is she eating right? Does she sleep enough? Should we move her to her own bed or let her continue to share with us? Our biggest concerns were raising a healthy baby and getting enough sleep.

It didn't take long for us to realize that we needed to be near family if we were going to have the support we needed while raising our child. So, we decided to move to my hometown of Glendale, California as soon as we had both finished school.

Micaela was almost a year old when we moved from Connecticut to California, and she was developing on a seemingly typical path. She was active and interested in the world around her, and she was meeting the expected physical milestones on time. We were too inexperienced to recognize her challenges with meeting important communication milestones. It wasn't until we'd been living in California for several months that we experienced any feelings of concern about our child's development.

At her one-year check up, our new pediatrician expressed concern that Micaela didn't speak many single words. At that time, she spoke only four words, including "mama" and "dada," which apparently don't actually count that much. We weren't worried.

At the eighteen-month visit, the pediatrician was concerned that she still only spoke a handful of single words. I told my husband that the doctor needed to stop pressuring our child; we didn't care if she wasn't bound for Harvard. However, it was around this time that we really started observing other children of Micaela's age. It wasn't the number of words they spoke that was so striking, it was the clear intent and focus of their communication, both verbal and non-verbal. They got their parents' attention and pointed at objects in the environment, then smiled back at their moms and dads. They grabbed items off of shelves and brought them back for their parents to see. With their words and their body language, these children invited communication and demanded interaction. They initiated and responded to social exchanges. Our daughter didn't do this.

Micaela was very well behaved, which is possibly why we didn't sense any problems. She could entertain herself quietly for indefinite periods of time. She never made demands. She could be mischievous, but never "naughty." She couldn't intentionally misbehave because our reactions were never a thought in her mind, as far as we could tell. It's almost as though she wasn't thinking about us at all unless we put ourselves directly and intentionally in her path and forced a reaction. When we did this, she might laugh or complain or make a demand, but we didn't know enough to make this type of interaction a priority. We were complacent and content with the relative peace our "easy baby" brought us.

Between one and a half and two years of age, our only real concerns were that Micaela was *very* active and that she did not seem to appreciate cuddles; once she was mobile, we had to sneak in our desperate snuggles while she was sleeping.

At the two-year visit, the doctor was more insistent. By then, Micaela spoke maybe a few dozen single words and no phrases. She used language to label things rather than to communicate. She also didn't use any nonverbal communication. She didn't point or nod or shake her head. When she wanted something, she did not try to get anyone's attention; she just kept trying to accomplish her goal on her own while mumbling or babbling to herself. The doctor made it clear that this was not typical language development and referred us to an evaluation with our local regional center. This was the official beginning of our adventures with autism.

After contacting the regional center, the first thing that we dealt with was testing… lots and lots of testing. Initially, it was a developmental specialist who came to our home to meet with us and evaluate Micaela. He referred us for a speech and language evaluation and an occupational therapy assessment. Each of those professionals came to our home as well. Finally, after getting the results of all of this testing, much of which placed Micaela's skills well below the average range for a child of her age, we were referred to a developmental psychologist.

The entire process, from referral to diagnosis, took about five months, but, overall, working with the regional center was very easy. Every assessment was free of charge. The therapists always came to our home and were extremely friendly and professional. When Micaela qualified for a therapy, services began almost immediately. By the time we went to visit the developmental psychologist, we were fairly prepared for a diagnosis on the autism spectrum. Hearing that our daughter's communication skills were below the first percentile, and getting a closer look, through the evaluation and therapy process, at how her skills compared to those of other kids her age really laid the foundation and gave us a lot of information to investigate and explore. We'd had enough time to observe her in new settings and to do some research. This made the actual diagnosis, when it came, unsurprising.

I am, however, embarrassed to say that I argued with the developmental psychologist when she suggested that a diagnosis of autism was appropriate for Micaela. I argued that my daughter's language skills were not yet delayed enough, and that she really only met criteria in two out of the three domains required for a diagnosis of autistic disorder: impaired social communication and repetitive behaviors.

I will admit that the diagnosis of autism frightened me. I tried to convince the psychologist that it was actually more appropriate to diagnose Micaela with Asperger's. In my mind, autism was a scary prospect. To me, that diagnosis didn't come with any optimism. Asperger's made me imagine Micaela growing up to be a quirky computer nerd in Silicon Valley who could make millions and provide her loving and supportive parents with a life of financial ease. Autism brought to mind pictures of a child, adolescent, and adult who would forever be dependent on us and always be limited in her communication and social skills. My understanding has obviously come a long way since then, and it's rather embarrassing to remember my mindset at that time. As it is, it was a blessing that the psychologist insisted that a diagnosis of autism was most appropriate.

I didn't know it at the time, but an autism diagnosis was required in order to qualify Micaela to receive regional center services. These are services that benefit our family to this day, and it is so reassuring to know that we have the support of this agency as Micaela matures and grows; once a part of the regional center system, she has access to the support that they offer for the rest of her life.

At the age of two and a half, the services Micaela had qualified to receive were quite extensive. I had no idea that so much support was available to families of children with developmental disabilities. Based on the evaluations that they had conducted, Micaela qualified for full-time preschool, weekly speech therapy, and weekly occupational therapy, and this was all at no cost to our family. In addition, she qualified for disability-based health insurance and respite services, which essentially provided several hours a week of in-home childcare.

While all of these services sound wonderful, and we were extremely grateful, taking advantage of this support was not without its challenges. We were selective about the types of environments we wanted for Micaela and cautious about placing her in just *any* preschool or with just *any* speech and language pathologist. We did a lot of research to find the right fits for our family, and, as often happens when working with public agencies, staff turnover was high with almost every therapy. This means that the process of meeting and introducing Micaela and her needs to new service coordinators, speech therapists, OTs, and caregivers was ongoing and a little frustrating when our goals were to help our daughter build social connections and to place her education and care in the hands of trusted individuals.

When we moved from Los Angeles County to Ventura County, the challenges grew. We had to deal with a new regional center and, because Micaela turned three shortly after our move, many of the early intervention services were discontinued, and responsibility for most of her ongoing learning needs was passed on to our new school district. This meant more assessments, more therapies, more decisions, and the added stress of IEP meetings that could last hours. We quickly realized that we needed to hire a special education advocate to help us make sense of everything.

All of this was very confusing and we became aware that, if Micaela was to continue making progress at the rate we hoped for, we would need to supplement many of the services she received by investing in private therapists. We often wished we were one of those wealthy families who could hire a group of trained professionals to help us address our daughter's many needs and collaborate on approaches designed to maximize her growth through a team approach. I wanted a homeschool and a gym and daily speech therapy and social skills classes, all staffed by gifted therapists and educators. As it was, we had to cobble together and coordinate a program that we felt would be successful, and we did this by utilizing a combination of public resources and private therapies.

At three years old, Micaela's program included enrollment in a phenomenal special education preschool, funded by the school district and just blocks from our new home. There, Micaela participated in small-group classes designed to develop her academic, language, and motor skills in an afternoon program taught by specialists, three days a week. In addition, we paid for her to attend a Montessori school five mornings a week. In this nurturing, child-directed learning environment, Micaela could play alongside typically developing peers and be challenged intellectually in support of her many academic strengths which included reading, writing, spelling, and memory for new information. Social skills were addressed through work with an agency funded by the regional center. Each week, instructors would spend time with Micaela facilitating play with her peers. We also paid for her to ride horses at a therapeutic riding facility; they worked on language, sensory, and motor skills during her weekly riding lessons. Private piano lessons, at our home, used a behavioral approach to teaching music while developing communication skills.

Every activity or therapy we pursued was sought with the intention of rounding out our daughter's daily program of learning in order to maximize her growth while keeping her in engaging, natural settings. This was not easy. Every therapist spent time with me and my husband explaining techniques and giving us pointers on how to integrate the therapy into our home lives. While it has been time-consuming, expensive, and labor intensive, I believe that this is the process that ultimately supported the amazing growth Micaela has experienced over the last decade. Over the years, her educational program has included:

- Montessori School
- Special Education Preschool
- Applied Behavioral Analysis
- Speech Therapy
- Occupational Therapy
- Sensory Integration Therapy
- Language Intervention
- Integrated Play Groups
- Therapeutic Riding
- Piano Lessons using Pivotal Response Training
- Communication Summer Camp
- Social Skills Summer Camp
- Hanen (More Than Words) Parent Training
- Social Thinking Classes

Through it all, we never felt discouraged, and we always talked openly with Micaela about her strengths and challenges. Despite my initial reaction, autism has never been a dirty word in our household. It is a word we use in the same way we talk about straight hair, brown eyes, height, weight, coordination, and glasses. In our home, autism is not a quality that is good or bad; autism is just one of the many facets of our daughter's being.

We always wanted to raise our child to be confident, self aware, resilient, independent, and compassionate. When Micaela was diagnosed, we worried that autism might make this task difficult, but we never assumed that it would be impossible. We never mourned the "loss" of our child because, to us, she is the same beautiful human being that she was on the day she was born. The challenges along the way have made each of her accomplishments all the more exciting and rewarding. As it is, our amazing child has made our original parenting mission more than possible- she's made it a reality far earlier than we anticipated. I hope you enjoy her perspective on her journey through childhood!

GLOSSARY

By Micaela Ellis

Autism: A developmental disability that involves a delay in communication and social skills

ADHD: Attention Deficit/Hyperactivity Disorder; a disorder that includes impulsivity and poor focus skills (not paying attention in class, getting bored with a task before finishing, difficulty following directions, making careless mistakes, etc.)

Puppy Love: When two people say they love each other (common with little kids), but their romantic relationship is shallow

Spork: A combination of a spoon and a fork

Big Side: The side of the Montessori campus that the big kids use for learning and playing

Little Side: The side of the Montessori campus that the little kids use for learning and playing

Inset: A metal stencil shape that is used for tracing and coloring

Golden Beads: A visual tool used for understanding place value in math

15

Chapter 1

Different

Call me different, call me special,
I'm just another imperfect human being.

My name is Micaela Rose Ellis. I was born in New Britain, Connecticut on September 21, 2005. I lived there, until I was almost one, with Mom, Dad, and my black cat named Princess (who is actually a boy). For about eleven months, Mom, Dad, and I lived in Connecticut. During that time, they realized that they needed the support of family and close friends to raise a child. We moved to Mom's hometown in California, and we lived there for almost two years.

As my mom and dad raised me for the first two years, they found that I talked less than other kids my age. After that, I got diagnosed with autism. Autism is something that people can get diagnosed with when they don't talk as much and often get fixated on specific topics.

I only knew four words at the time: Mama, Dada, cat, and a bad word that starts with "sh." I knew Mama and Dada because my parents taught me what to call them. I knew the word "cat" because I had Princess, and I learned the "sh" word from Mom and Dad because they sometimes used bad language without knowing that I was going to repeat their words.

I have this faint memory of walking around my bedroom in Glendale, in the dark, when I was two. Mom or Dad must have put me in there to nap. I am not a good napper, even now.

I don't remember talking much when I was little. As a two-year-old, I usually played by myself when I was around other kids, except for my best friend at the time, Macie. Though we played together, I didn't talk to Macie that much. She had this little kiddie pool we would splash in, and I had lots of fun with her on our playdates. That ended when my family moved to Oxnard, California.

When we moved to Oxnard, I was almost three

and just learning how to swim. At my new house, there was a pool, a hot tub, a big house where my grandpa, Pop-Pop, lives (he invited us to live with him), a smaller house where my family lives, a tennis court, a guest cottage (kind of like a studio apartment), a cute little house that you can walk in called the playhouse, and a bunch of land on the one-acre property.

Mom and Dad enrolled me in a Montessori school which is half an hour from our home. Montessori was a good school to start with; Montessori classrooms have this way of organizing things so that kids can walk around the room. This really helps with ADHD (Attention Deficit/Hyperactivity Disorder), which I've also been diagnosed with. When you finish the work you have to do, you get to choose an activity called "Free Choice," like magnets, drawing, and stuff like that. For me, it was a rare treat to earn "Free Choice" because I had a hard time focusing on work.

In my classroom, there was nap-time, which meant you could nap on a little sleeping pad with sheets on it. My teacher at the time, Rachel, let me read books instead of napping because I was not a good napper.

By the time I was three, my parents found help from Creating Inclusive Opportunities (CIO), a program that helped with social skills. One of the people from CIO, Joan, sometimes came to Montessori with me to help me with my social skills.

Joan's method of helping me socialize with other kids was to create group games like Tag and Catch. Other times, I played with my school friends without Joan's assistance, but those times were very seldom. I only had a few playdates with other kids outside of school hours. Mom and Dad would set up playdates sometimes, but I didn't really care if I had playdates with other kids.

When I was in preschool, I never seemed to care if I was socializing or not. I seemed to like sitting next to the teachers at lunch instead of sitting with my classmates. I liked to play my own little quiet pretend games. For example, when I was about four, I played a game by myself where I would drive to work in my "car" (one of the trikes the school had), drive home, sleep in my bed at my "house" (a bottle-brush tree), wake up, go to work, and the cycle would continue.

One kid was annoyed that when I "parked" my "car," I would get frustrated when he tried to take it. The teacher got involved when she saw that I was keeping the trike to myself. She asked, "Are you going to ride the red trike or sleep in the tree?"

To the teacher, it looked like I wanted to sleep in the tree and not ride the trike, so she told the kid who wanted to use the trike that he could use it.

As a response, I ran to the red trike that the kid was now using, but the teacher stopped me. She said to me, "Somebody gets off, somebody gets on."

But I was playing a game. I needed that to get to work in my game! I thought. If I didn't have autism, I might have said, "I need that trike to drive to work in my game! I park my car by my house so I can go to sleep at my house! Then I'll wake up and get in my car and drive to work." I'd maybe have played that game with other kids; I might have been a mom in the game who had kids who would go to school. All of that could have happened if I didn't have autism, and I might have had other cool social experiences too. But, at the time, I didn't have the mindset to make these things happen.

The teacher got involved when she saw that
I was keeping the trike to myself.

Chapter 2

My New Disc Swing

One day, I was waiting for my dad to pick me up from the Assistance League School. Assistance League School is a place in Oxnard where I would work on my motor skills and my social skills. I still went to the Montessori school, but the Assistance League School was an afternoon program that I did.

Dad drove his truck over to the Assistance League campus, and I got in. He said to me, "I have something for you at the house!"

What is it? I wondered.

"It's a disc swing!" Dad told me. I didn't know what a disc swing was, but I was excited to find out.

Dad and I got home, and then we walked into our house. On the floor, I saw a box with a picture of a kid swinging on a round, yellow disc attached to a rope. My swing!

Dad cut open the tape that sealed the package, and then I saw an owner's manual and a rope attached to a disc to sit on. I smiled, and Dad took me outside to find a good tree for the disc swing. We passed the tennis court and passed avocado trees and, finally, we found the perfect tree for the rope and swing to hang from.

While Dad set up my swing, I put one foot on a tree and the other on the wall that created a border between our property and the neighbor's property. For the one second I was there, I saw my neighbor's house, play structure, and pool. *They have a pool just like me,* I thought. I wanted to observe more about my neighbor's backyard, so I tried to climb the tree.

"Your swing is ready," Dad said to me.

I got onto the swing, and then Dad asked me, "Are you ready?"

"Yes!" I said.

I clung to the rope on my swing as Dad pushed me high into the air. I saw the ground below me, and my heart filled with joy as I was taken closer and closer to the sky. Dad knew that I liked when he pushed me high into the air, so he pushed me more and more until his arms got tired. I had a lot of fun that day, and I realized that I was the proud owner of a disc swing.

Chapter 3

I Swallowed a Feather
(and Other Random Actions & Ideas)

When I was a little kid, I made up some strange ideas in my head. One of them was that if I swallowed a small goose feather from my couch, I was going to teleport to a place called Vertical Heaven. Vertical Heaven was a place in Ventura that was for climbing and other fitness-related activities. I enjoyed the environment there; it was a spacious, busy room with people doing different activities.

I took a feather from my sofa, put it in my mouth, and swallowed it. It felt tickly and uncomfortable when it went down my throat, and then tears came into my eyes. I started crying because the feather was in my throat, and I couldn't get it out. Mom got off the couch and asked me, "Are you okay?"

I choked out, "I swallowed a feather."

I wasn't actually choking, but I felt a lump of sadness creep into my throat. I was still at my house, my throat felt tickly and dry, and I was miserable.

I had thought that I was going to teleport to Vertical Heaven and have fun climbing the rock wall there, but my feet were still on the green rug of my living room and not on the gray carpet of the Vertical Heaven floor.

"I'll go get you some water to wash it down," Mom told me.

In her mind, she probably felt confused because I swallowed a feather. She went into the kitchen to fill a cup of water for me. She came back with a plastic cup with water and ice in it. She handed me my water, and I took the time to drink it. I drank my water from the small cup until there were only a few droplets left. As the cold water rushed down my throat, I felt better. I wasn't climbing the rock wall at Vertical Heaven, but Mom's warm, comforting hugs made up for it.

If I was like other four-year-old kids and didn't have autism, I probably wouldn't have swallowed a feather. Instead, I might have said, "Mommy! Daddy!

Can you please take me to Vertical Heaven? Pleeeeease?" But I had challenges with communicating my thoughts, so I didn't have the words to tell Mom why I swallowed a feather until eight years after that happened.

~*~

In class, I drew a picture. I drew myself as a six-year-old, but I had blonde hair. I came up with the idea that I was going to have blonde hair as soon as I turned six, and I stuck with that idea. I thought that, on my sixth birthday, I was going to wake up with blonde hair. I daydreamed about my six-year-old life with blonde hair, and I was positive that this was going to happen. My belief that I would eventually have blonde hair stuck with me until I woke up on my sixth birthday with the same dark-brown hair I had fallen asleep with.

Later, I drew myself as a teenager. In this picture, I had black hair, and I was standing next to a ladder. This idea makes more sense than the first two I mentioned. I thought Mom had black hair, but I found out later that Mom actually has dark-brown hair, not black hair. I wanted to be like Mom, so that is the reason why I thought I was going to have black hair. I eventually forgot about this idea when Mom told me that she had dark-brown hair.

As a girl with autism, I didn't have the words to tell anyone about what I thought in my head. I just kept my thoughts and ideas inside, but I didn't care whether anyone else knew or didn't know what I was thinking.

Another idea I made up in my head was that I was going to turn into a baby on my tenth birthday. I thought that I was going to teleport back to New Britain, Connecticut, where I was born. I imagined that years after I was reborn, when I turned twelve, I'd go back to Glendale and then move to Oxnard, where I'd be thirteen (a teenager). I believed this until I was five, and then I dismissed this idea too.

Eight years later, at age twelve, I told Mom about my idea where I was going to turn back into a baby. She laughed so hard. She asked me, "Where did you come up with that idea?"

I told her, "I just came up with it in my head at the time."

Chapter 4

Ballet and its Bad Ending

I was four years old, and I was on summer break. I started off the summer with painting classes at the Barranca Vista Community Center in Ventura. The room where I painted had a table and chairs around it, and I painted there with the other kids. Painting was a lot of fun; I just painted whatever came to my mind.

After painting ended, my parents signed me up for ballet. They told me that I was going to do ballet, and I just couldn't wait to start. They purchased a ballet dress for me and got ballet slippers from the store. I had my ballet dress and ballet shoes. I was all set!

At my ballet class, I met the other students and my teacher, Geraldine. According to my dad, Geraldine wasn't very patient with me, but I enjoyed ballet anyway. I never noticed Geraldine's impatience; I was too absorbed in what I was doing to notice.

I don't remember all the girls' names in my ballet class, but I do remember a girl named Chelsea, who didn't seem very nice in the end.

I remember dancing with Chelsea and the other girls. We were princesses by a lake, and we were supposed to be dancing gracefully. I imagined lots of princesses in white dresses dancing in the evening. I was going to be one of the princesses. I leaped to the end of the room with everyone, and I leaped back to where I started as Geraldine played a CD for us to dance to.

After ballet, a person from CIO, Rhonda, would pick me up and play with me on the playground until Dad came to get me. She and I would sit together and she'd talk to me.

One day, I was with Rhonda, and I saw Chelsea's sister. I knew she was Chelsea's older sister because she looked like Chelsea, only older. She had the same blonde hair and pale skin that Chelsea had, but her hair was short and wavy while Chelsea's was medium length and straight. She said, "I'm Jill," to someone who wasn't me. I saw Jill and Chelsea's mom and, for some reason, I thought their mom's name was Jill also.

~*~

I woke up and got ready as usual. I did all the normal stuff to get ready for ballet, and then I realized I couldn't find my ballet slippers. Where were my ballet slippers? I cried and cried until Dad grabbed me some hot-pink flats and rushed me out the door to drive to ballet.

When we got to the building, I saw that the room was set up with chairs in rows and a space for the ballet students to dance for the showcase. I saw my dad take a seat, I saw other parents, and I saw Chelsea's mom.

Right as the showcase was about to begin, I walked up to Chelsea's mom and asked her, "What's your name?"

Chelsea's mom said, "My name is Beatrice."

"What did you say to my mommy!?" Chelsea demanded rudely.

I didn't know what to say. I buried my face in

my knees and arms and sat in a corner of the room and cried. What was I going to do? Chelsea was mad at me! All I did was ask Chelsea's mom what her name was!

I decided to never do ballet there again if Chelsea was going to be there. In my head, Chelsea was mean to snap at me like that. In the real world, Chelsea did nothing wrong; she felt suspicious about what I had said to her mom. I didn't do anything wrong either; I just asked Chelsea's mom what her name was. I took Chelsea's question the wrong way. I thought she was mad at me. If I didn't have autism, I might have stood up for myself and said something like, "I just asked your mom what her name was!"

Nobody knew what went on in my head that day. People probably thought that, for some reason, I suddenly didn't like ballet. In fact, I didn't like doing ballet anymore. I hated doing it because I thought that Chelsea was mean to me. I didn't have the words to tell anyone why I sat in a corner of the room and cried.

Chapter 5

A New School Year

That watercolor paint set! So new and fresh looking! I wanted to paint with it so badly! I was almost five, and I was visiting the classroom that I was going to be in for kindergarten. It looked so clean and fresh! A fresh new school year with fresh watercolor paints. I was so excited!

"Those are for when school starts," Maria, my teacher, said. She had seen me looking at the paints. Then I looked around the classroom to find something to do. School would not be starting until the next day. Dad had brought me to Montessori with him because he had to work in the garden. Dad was the garden teacher at Montessori.

"Go outside and play," Maria said. She needed me out of the classroom so she could set up for the next day. The next day was the first day of school. I was excited to get back to school. I thought that I had stopped going to school for good because I was gone from school for such a long time.

I missed the loft in the classroom where I'd sit and read with my head on the soft pillows. The year before, I would enjoy walking around the school play yard and seeing my reflection walking in the classroom windows next to me. That day, I entertained myself at school until Dad took me home.

At home, I played with my toys, had dinner, got ready for bed, and fell asleep.

The next day, I woke up, put on my dress, ate breakfast, brushed my hair, brushed my teeth, and then got in the truck to wait for Dad to drive me to school.

When I got to school, Dad signed me in, and we walked into my classroom. I saw some new kids and some of my classmates from other school years. I saw Courtney, who was also new to Maria's class. Like me, she had come from Rachel's class. I remember meeting Donald for the first time, and I remember meeting Talise as well. Donald and Talise were both new at Montessori, and I really liked Talise.

Talise and I were about the same age, but I was older by a few months. She had light-brown hair, tan skin, purple glasses, and I remember that she smiled a lot. Donald was six years old, and he had dirty-blonde hair and pale skin. He was a bit chubby, and I didn't know him very well.

At lunchtime, all the hot-lunch kids lined up on one side of the room, while the kids who brought their own lunches lined up on the other side. I was in the hot-lunch line, and all of the hot-lunch kids would run to the kitchen to fill their hungry bellies with the foods of their choice.

Kids would line up outside of the kitchen and wait their turn to get their food. For my turn, I stepped onto the stool to look at my choices of food. For hot lunch, there was always a main dish and then lots of side items at the counter.

At the counter, I saw my choices of side items. My choices were banana chips, peanuts, peanut butter, vanilla yogurt, cottage cheese, celery, olives, pineapple pieces, applesauce, string cheese pieces, raisins, and some other foods. I ordered the things I liked: yogurt, cheese sticks, peanut butter, banana chips, and applesauce. I took a spork and my paper plate, which was filled with the main dish and the side items I liked.

I ate my lunch, and then I asked a teacher, "Can I be done?"

"Yes, you can be done," the teacher said.

I went to the play structure and played a game by myself until someone rang a bell for the kids from my class to go inside. I went back to class with the other kids and had my fun in the loft in the classroom. I read books as I leaned my head on a pillow.

There were some interesting books there. There were books about nature, animals, and other fascinating topics. I also liked to look at myself in the loft mirror. I'd see a girl with brown hair and brown eyes staring back at me.

Other kids in my class were doing their work. Some were using the golden beads to work with large numbers up to the thousands place, others were on Free Choice doing whatever fun things they wanted, and other kids were writing in their workbooks. Nobody but me was exploring the loft.

I also went to the bean bags in the space under the loft, and I would see "Tommy" written in permanent marker on the wood. I wondered who "Tommy" was, but I didn't have the words to express my thoughts. Autism has those downsides. Kids with autism may seem like they don't have a lot going through their brains, but a lot went through my mind at the time.

I processed a lot of information as a kid, but I didn't know how to share my thoughts with others. If I was a kid who didn't have autism, I might have asked the teacher, "Who's Tommy?" Instead, I just kept quiet, like usual. That was how my normal school day went.

Another day, I found an old workbook of mine in my kindergarten class. It was from when I was three. It was on a shelf, and it had a blue cover that said, "Tim and Bear." I opened *Tim and Bear* up, and I saw all of my old coloring. There was a story on each page, and I remembered how, when I was three, I would follow the instructions that were printed on the page. On one of the pages was written, "Color the bear yellow. Color Ann orange. Color Tim red. Color the cat brown."

I decided to work on this book in my new class. When I finished a page, I showed Maria's assistant, Josephine, my work. Josephine checked my work and she marked it with a green pencil.

I liked Josephine. She would call me "Ann" from the workbook when she was playing around with me, but she'd call me Micaela when she needed me to follow her directions.

I liked being called Ann when I was with Josephine. I liked it because I felt I had someone who understood me. It was like an inside joke; it was something that only the two of us understood. It was my first time having a special bond with someone outside of my family.

Chapter 6

I Got in Trouble Sometimes, But Was it My Fault?

It was during Circle Time when I got in trouble. In my mind, Donald was the reason I got in trouble. Maria called all the kids to the circle and read a story to the class. Donald decided to sing a song that went, "Time to, time to brush my teeth!" While he sang, he made movements with his hand as if he were brushing his teeth. Thinking I had to, I joined in with Donald and we both sang together.

Maria stopped what she was doing so she could say, "Shhhhhh!"

"Time to, time to brush my teeth!" Donald sang.

"Time to, time to brush my teeth!" I joined in.

"Shhhhhhhh!" Maria said.

"Time to, time to brush my teeth!" Donald whisper-sang.

"Time to, time to brush my teeth!" I joined in.

Maria's voice boomed to me, "Go to that table and put your head down!" and she gestured to a table.

"Time to, time to brush my teeth!" Donald still whisper-sang. I went to a table, put my head down and cried.

I felt that it wasn't fair that I got in trouble while Donald got off scot-free. Why did I have to put my head down while Donald still got to be in the circle, even though he started singing "Time to, time to brush my teeth!" before me?

I knew Maria had said to stop singing while she was reading a story, but since Donald was singing, I thought I had to sing too. If I didn't have autism, and I was singing with Donald when Maria told me to put my head down, I might have said, "Why aren't you making Donald put his head down too? He was the kid that started singing first!" Maybe if I didn't have autism, I would have stopped singing when the teacher said to.

When I first joined Maria's class, I learned that I had to ask someone if I could be excused to go to the bathroom. All of the other kids knew that "someone" meant the teacher in the classroom, but I thought that you could just ask anyone in the classroom if you could go to the bathroom.

One day, when I was in class, I had to go to the bathroom. I ran to the door and, just as I opened the door, I asked a boy by the door, "Can I go to the bathroom?" He stood there baffled, and, before he said anything, I ran out the door into the hall and to the girls' bathroom.

The hall with the classrooms, bathroom, and kitchen wasn't exactly a hall. The hall was a concrete floor with no walls preventing you from going outside, but there were walls and doors separating the hall from the classrooms. There were also eaves coming from the roof of the building that covered the concrete floor.

When I got to the bathroom, I heard Maria yelling from behind me, "Mickey, I'm very disappointed in you!" Mickey was what everyone called me.

"You were supposed to ask a teacher if you could go to the bathroom, not a classmate!" Maria boomed at me.

I had no response. I came out of the bathroom stall, washed my hands, and then exited the girls' bathroom to get a paper towel.

I saw Maria outside the bathroom with a cross look on her face. She marched me to Rachel's classroom, which was my old preschool classroom. Tears were streaming from my eyes as Maria opened the preschool classroom door. Rachel was singing a song with the preschoolers as I sobbed and wailed loudly. She continued singing with the kids, despite my loud crying. After the song ended, Rachel said to me, "I'm very disappointed in you, Mickey."

But I didn't know, I thought. I got in trouble but it wasn't my fault. The kid I had asked permission from to go to the bathroom maybe thought it was weird that I had asked him. If I was like the other kids my age, I wouldn't have taken it literally when Maria said that you had to ask "someone" if you could go to the bathroom. I would've known to ask a teacher if I could go to the bathroom, not a classmate. But I have autism, and I can't change the fact that sometimes I take things too literally.

~*~

One time, Mom and Dad had Granny and Grandpa Alvin come from Alabama to visit for a few days. Pop-Pop had them and my family over for dinner. At dinner, Dad mentioned the garden sign that he made that said what to put in the compost pile and what not to put in. I added to the conversation, "Poop and feces, not allowed!"

Mom got annoyed and took me outside of Pop-Pop's house. She gave me a lecture on how I shouldn't talk about poop and feces in front of Pop-Pop, Granny, and Grandpa Alvin. When I said "Poop and feces, not allowed!" at the dinner table, I was talking about the sign for the compost pile. It said that feces weren't supposed to go in the compost pile. If I didn't have autism, I might've said to Mom, "But Mom, it says on Dad's garden sign that poop and feces aren't allowed in the compost pile!"

~*~

One day, I woke up to the thought of eating cookies that I had gotten the night before. The night before, I had been at a Christmas party that Pop-Pop had at his house. I had gotten chocolate chip cookies in a bag, but I had already had enough sweets that night. In the morning, I went into Mom and Dad's room and asked Mom, "Can I eat my cookies?"

Mom answered groggily, "You can eat them at 9:00."

I left the room and looked at my clock that hung on the wall. The second hand passed the 9 and I was about to leave the room to get my cookies. Then, the second hand passed the 10, 11, 12, 1, 2, 3, 4, 5, 6, 7, 8, and then the 9 again. I went into Mom and Dad's room, and I asked Mom again, "Now can I have cookies?"

Mom answered again, "At 9:00," and I left.

I watched the clock some more and, again, I went back to Mom and Dad's room. Mom asked me, "Is it 9:00?"

I said, uncertain, "Yes."

I didn't know what time it was. I thought that it was 9:00 every time the second hand passed the 9 on a clock. In my mind, it could have been 9:00, 10:00, or 12:00. I went to the kitchen and grabbed my bag of cookies from the top of the microwave. I sat at the table in my living room and happily munched my cookies.

"Micaela Rose!" I heard Mom call.

I ran to Mom and Dad's room, and I saw Mom's angry face.

"You weren't supposed to eat cookies! It's not 9:00! I asked you, 'Is it 9:00?' and you answered, 'Yes.' You were being dishonest!"

But it was 9:00. I wasn't being dishonest! I thought. If I didn't have autism, I might have said, "It was 9:00! It was 9:00 so many times today! When I said 'Yes' when you asked me if it was 9:00, I didn't know if it was 9:00!"

Mom would have told me that it would be 9:00 every time the hour hand was on the nine, not every time the second hand passed the nine. Instead, I wasn't able to express my thoughts to anyone, and I kept my thoughts in my head while I got in trouble.

Chapter 7

Getting Prepared

As a five-year-old, I didn't need to be on the little-kid side of the Montessori campus anymore. All the stuff my classmates were learning, I already knew. I already knew how to read and write, I already knew how to add and subtract. I needed more academic challenge; the *Tim and Bear* workbook I had found a couple months back was way too simple for me.

Mom and Dad told me about transitioning from Maria's class to Laura's, which was on the big side. When I was riding home with Mom and Dad, Mom said to me, "I have something great to tell you!"

I looked at her.

"You're going to be in Laura's class on the big side!" Mom said.

"I'm so proud of you! You're now a big girl!" Dad said.

I was so excited! I felt butterflies in my stomach! I would have more privileges on the big side than on the little side. The big kids got to run and ride trikes on the field. The little kids didn't even have a field. Also, the big kids were old enough to learn more complicated sports for PE, like kickball, basketball, tennis, baseball, badminton, and soccer.

On the big side, the big kids could chant, "Little kid attack! Little kid attack!" as the kids from the little side would march to the blacktop in order to do sports with the PE teacher, Mike. I didn't know how lucky I was to have these advantages, but I was excited to go onto the big side all the same.

At Montessori, kids would visit classrooms a few times before moving up. I was in class one day when Josephine said to me, "Time to visit Laura's class!"

I grabbed my *Tim and Bear* workbook, my addition and subtraction workbook, and a pencil from my cubby. With these things in hand, I walked down the hall with Josephine. She opened the gate that divided the big side of the campus and the little side. We walked down the hall, and I saw the door of Laura's classroom. It was red and had the room number painted on it in white.

I pushed open the door and stepped into the room. It was a large room with wooden cubbies for all the students. The desks were arranged to face a white dry-erase board. There was a desk for the teacher and a table for the assistant to sit at. There was a reading corner with lots of books and some chairs to sit on. There were metal stencils of different shapes (called insets), Prismacolor colored pencils, school supplies on shelves, cupboards of supplies, a rug to sit on during circle time, a shelf holding small carpet squares that were each big enough for a child to sit on, and a glass-top table with light showing through from underneath.

There was also a counter with a sink, a water jug, a dish rack, plates, cups, and washcloths that kids brought for themselves from home. There was a shelf with snacks that teachers provided for the kids. In this classroom, kids were allowed to eat in class, and the teacher would wash your plate when you were done. By the sink, there were also paper towels and washcloths for kids to use after they used the sink.

I then heard a cheerful voice say to me, "You used to call me Llama!" It was my soon-to-be teacher, Laura!

"Hi, Laura!" I said. Laura was going to be my new teacher, and I was excited to start!

Llama was what I called Laura when I was three, and I remember that every time I saw her I'd say, "Hi, Llama!"

Once, when Mom, Dad, and I were in the car and leaving the Montessori campus, I yelled out the window, "Bye, Llama!" as we passed Laura. Laura didn't get mad at me for calling her Llama. I think she thought it was funny.

As I stood in the classroom with Laura and Josephine, I saw some of my classmates from the year before and some of my classmates from previous school years, like Celes, Maddyson, Alana, and Kai. Alana and Kai weren't very nice in my opinion, but they weren't very nice in different ways.

Alana was physically a bully. She hit, scratched, and pushed her classmates. Kai was a different case. He was merely bratty and rude.

Laura let me sit at her desk. I opened my *Tim and Bear* workbook; I started coloring in it and didn't stop until my visit ended. Then, I went back to Maria's classroom with the assistant, Josephine, and I continued my work there.

On one of my last days in Maria's classroom, I asked Maria if I could go to the bathroom. She let me go, and I walked to the girls' bathroom. I entered the bathroom, grabbed a stool from below a sink, went into a stall, and sat down to use the toilet.

A moment later, Courtney walked into the bathroom and crawled under my stall door, smiling. She had a tube of glittery fuschia lip gloss in one hand and the lid for it in the other. She had lip gloss on her lips and was going to put some on me.

Courtney applied the lip gloss to my lips and smiled. I smiled also, and we exited the bathroom, snickering.

We got to class and I looked in the mirror above the classroom sink. I saw the brown-haired girl smiling back at me with her lips pink and sparkly. After that, I continued my classwork.

Courtney was nice to put lip gloss on me, but we weren't going to be able to be friends for a while, since she and I would be in different classes for a long time. If I didn't have autism, and my social skills were better, I might have gotten to know Courtney better. We could have had playdates and we could have been close friends, even though we were in different classes. Instead, I didn't become friends with Courtney until later; however, I know now that she wasn't a very good friend for me anyway.

Chapter 8

A Holiday Train Ride

Mom, Dad, and I were off to Toppers Pizza Place in Ventura. After dinner, we were going on a holiday train ride with Santa! I was quiet on the car ride there, but Mom and Dad filled the silence with their conversation.

Dad parked the car, and we met up with Andrew, Sadie, and their dad, Kevin. Andrew and Sadie's mom, Jamie, had stuff to do that night, so she couldn't come to Toppers or go on the train ride. I would always call Jamie by the name Jamie Patterson because Mom has a lot of books by the author James Patterson.

My family and Andrew's family sat at a booth, and I asked Dad if I could be excused to go to the bathroom. Dad let me go, and he gave me my Rapunzel nightgown to put on. He pointed to the bathroom sign so I could see where the bathroom was.

I went to the bathroom and put on my Rapunzel nightgown. I was going on a night-time train ride with Sadie and Andrew, and we were all wearing our pajamas. I came back to our booth and saw the hot pizza on the table. I sat next to Andrew and Sadie, and we ate our pizza.

After we ate our pizza, Andrew's family walked to their car while my family and I walked to ours. Dad put the keys in the ignition, and he drove us off to the Fillmore and Western station for our train ride with Santa.

When we got to the train station, we met up with Andrew's family and walked to our train. We stood in a long line of people boarding the train, and it felt like forever. Finally, it was our turn to board the train.

My family sat at a table with Andrew's family. I heard the engine start; we were finally leaving Fillmore behind! A man dressed up as Santa Claus came to our booth. I was sitting on Dad's lap, squirming with excitement. I saw Santa Man out of the corner of my eye, and I was wriggling and wriggling while Dad tried to keep me still. If I didn't have autism, I might have paid more attention to Santa Man, and I maybe would have said something close to, "Hi Santa! Guess what? I'm in my pajamas!" Instead, I wiggled and stared out the window instead of looking at Santa Man.

I knew that the man wasn't actually Santa Claus, but it was exciting to see a man dressed up as Santa Claus. Dad held me in his lap, but I kept squirming. Finally, I calmed down, but by the time I got to see Santa Man, he was already walking away.

I looked out the window, but I didn't see anything interesting, just the darkness of nighttime. The train ride flew by and, when it was over, we exited the train. We gave our hugs to Andrew's family and walked to the car. Dad drove us away from the train station.

I saw a mug in the backseat that had a Christmas wreath and a train design on it. The mug had capital letters in red that said, "2010 FILLMORE EXPRESS."

I liked the mug a lot and was excited to drink eggnog out of it. In the car, there were four mugs that looked like the one I saw: one for me, one for Mom, one for Dad, and an extra. Back at home, we only had the Corduroy Christmas mug, and I always wanted to drink eggnog from that mug at Christmastime.

The Corduroy mug didn't actually have Corduroy, the teddy bear from the books, on it, but I still called the mug a Corduroy mug. The mug had many different teddy bears on it, not just one. I thought that the bears on the mug were Corduroy's family, but I never told anyone that. Mom and Dad didn't know why I called it the Corduroy mug. I was still going to use the Corduroy mug, but I was also going to use my new train mug as well.

When we got home, I went into my room and got ready for bed. I went into the bathroom so I could brush my teeth. Then, I gave Mom and Dad hugs and kisses and went back to my room and got in bed. I fell fast asleep after my busy day.

I felt that my day was amazing. When I was wiggling around in Dad's lap, I didn't realize that nobody else was squirming around in the train but me. With autism, I couldn't really tell when it was the right time to do something and when it wasn't the right time.

Chapter 9

My First Week

I woke up and got ready for my first day in Laura's class. Dad and I got into his truck, and he drove me to school. When we got out, Dad walked me to my new classroom. I gave him a hug and a kiss, and I joined the classroom. It was fun and exciting at first, but I felt out of place for most of the week.

When I got inside the classroom, I grabbed my things from my new cubby, and I sat at a table. All of my old things were there, but, strangely, my *Tim and Bear* workbook was missing. I didn't know why it wasn't in my cubby, but I think my teacher took it out of my cubby because it was too simple for me.

I saw a few of my classmates from my previous classes, and I asked one of them, Emma, "How old are you?"

Emma answered, "Six." Then we both went

back to our work. Later, Laura called everyone to the circle. All of the kids in my class grabbed small mats, and Laura showed us something.

She announced to the class, "These are the book-making supplies. You need two pieces of construction paper, ten pieces of white paper, and the stapler is needed to keep the paper together. Here is a book I made." Laura showed us a small book she had made, and it had a yellow cover. I was pretty impressed, and I hoped to make a book.

After the announcement, it was time to eat snack. I ate my snack, and I then went to play on the playground. I played by myself until someone rang the bell.

When everyone in my class was inside, I headed straight to the book-making area. I chose two small, purple pieces of construction paper, ten small pieces of white paper, and markers I liked. I took these things to a table, and I started writing. I wrote on the cover, "Grapes and Eggs Talk." I don't remember what crazy things I wrote in that book, but I remember that I mentioned Kai in there. I put *Grapes and Eggs Talk* in my cubby, and I went to do other work.

I found a short book to read. The book was called *Being Careless*, by Joy Berry, and it was a book from the *Let's Talk About* series.

I started reading the book, and I liked it a lot. The book talked about why being careless is bad, and why nobody likes when people are careless. The book was illustrated with kids talking to each other and showed speech bubbles coming out of their mouths. I finished the book, and I put it back on the shelf.

After that, I continued working, and then it was time to go to lunch. The hot-lunch kids went to the kitchen and got lunch. I was one of the hot-lunch kids, and I got my food. I ate my lunch, and I asked a teacher if I could be done. The teacher said yes, and I went to play by myself on a play structure.

I came back, and I saw Laura holding a phone. It was an iPhone, and I had never seen an iPhone before then. It had an apple on it, and I saw that it said "iPhone."

I ran back to the play structure I liked, and I sang to myself in a whisper voice, "Phone, phone,

phone, phone." Nobody heard me, and I continued playing alone on the playground for the rest of recess.

A kid rang the bell for my class, and we all walked into the classroom. All of the desks were put in a semi-circle facing the white dry-erase board, and the students sat at their desks.

I sat at an empty desk, and Laura started talking. She said, "The earth has four layers. The top layer is the crust, and it is the part we live on. The second layer is the mantle, and it is very hot. The third layer is the outer core, and the fourth is the inner core." She showed us a visual that she had made and it had arrows that pointed to the different layers.

She continued to tell us more about the layers of the earth, all of which I don't remember, and then she dismissed us. Dad picked me up, and we went home together.

~*~

When I went back to school the next day, I went to the tower-like play structure I had played on the day before. Then I noticed something. Alana and Emma were standing together and playing with a beautiful yellow flower. I saw them walk away together, going to play something else.

I always played alone, but I felt content playing by myself. I was an only child, so I was used to playing alone. I played by myself until someone rang the bell, and I went in with the rest of the class to do work until PE.

For PE, we were going to play tennis. My class went outside, and then I spied the yellow flower Emma and Alana had been playing with earlier. I walked to the stone bench that it was laying on, and I picked it up. It was a tiny bit wilted, but otherwise it looked beautiful. I sat on the cold bench and admired the flower in my hand.

Other kids were playing tennis, but I was on the sidelines playing with a flower. I saw Alana walking towards me. She said, "Let me see that."

Innocently, I let her take the flower out of my hand. Any other five-year-old kid would have been able to tell that Alana was angry, but as a child with autism, I didn't understand that she was mad. I thought she just wanted to look at the flower that was in my hand.

Alana held the flower and, with her free hand, she slapped me and stormed off with the flower.

Her slap stung, and I felt miserable. If I didn't have autism, my initial reaction to her slapping me might have been to say, "Don't hit me! Go pick on somebody your own size!" Or maybe I would have thrown wood chips at her. Or instead, maybe none of this would have happened because I probably would have been playing tennis with my class.

I got up from the bench, and I saw the tennis teacher. I said to the teacher, "Alana hit me!"

The teacher didn't respond, but she helped me get started on playing tennis. My class played tennis until snack. I ate snack with Emma, Celes, and Maddyson. Emma was talking about how she saw *Winnie the Pooh*.

I said, "I saw *High School Musical* with my cousin, Jacob."

Emma said to me, "We're not talking about that."

Tears came into my eyes. I left the table, and I sat alone, crying. I felt that Emma was mean to me when she said that they weren't talking about *High School Musical.* If I didn't have autism, I might have given a response that was on topic like, "Did you like *Winnie the Pooh?*" I maybe would have been closer friends with Emma, Celes, and Maddyson.

When I got to class, I decided to read *Being Careless* again. I read it, and I put it back on the shelf. I felt more comfortable when things were predictable and familiar, so reading *Being Careless* a second time made me happy.

I think many people with autism feel this comfort because books stay the same, unlike people. It was easier for me to read books than it was to read people's expressions, so I felt a stronger connection with books than I did with people sometimes.

After reading, I grabbed a tray with the golden beads, and I took it to Laura's table. I didn't have a desk yet, so I would do my work at Laura's table. I did some math, and then I played with the beads for awhile. I then did more math, and I played with the beads some more. This was not really typical behavior for a child my age. Five-year-old kids can get distracted sometimes, but I would get distracted for long periods of time.

The beads were transparent and golden, hence their name. There were little individual beads, and there were beads connected in different combinations. There were small wire rods with ten beads wired onto them, thin, flat squares that had a hundred beads wired onto them, and cubes with a thousand beads wired onto them.

I played with these beads, and I then finished my math problems. I put the golden-bead tray back on the shelf, and I walked to a table to get inset supplies.

I took a shape I liked, a piece of paper, and some pencils, and I then started coloring inside the frame. I finished coloring, and I put my inset picture in my cubby. I put my supplies back, and I wandered around the classroom until lunch.

At lunch, I stood in the lunch line and ordered my food when it was my turn. I ate at a table alone, and then went off to play.

In the play area on the big side, there were many

things to play on. There was an oak tree that kids were allowed to climb, a set of six swings, the tower-like play structure that I liked, a larger play structure, monkey bars, a ball wall that older kids would play at, a tall metal slide, a small play structure with large hoops that swung, a small play structure that had a slide and steps, a small, wooden play house that could fit three elementary-school kids, a black-top that kids could ride trikes on, a large sandbox that contained all the play structures, and lots of grass to play on as well.

I went to the hoops and sat in one. I sat quietly for a minute, and I then made a noise with my mouth. "Tttttttttttttttttttttt," I went. As I made that noise, the world shook in my head. I thought other kids would notice that the world was shaking, but they still went on with their recess as if the world wasn't shaking.

I enjoyed making the noise that shook the world. "Tttttttttttttttttttttt," I went again. I thought that I was able to make the world shake, but outside of my mind, the world wasn't really shaking. I spent the rest of my recess at the hoop, and I went to class when the bell rang. After my final class, school was dismissed.

~*~

When I got to school the next day, I had art class, and I then had snack. I ate and played alone, and then I went back to class.

I was in class for a while until I had to go to the bathroom. Laura excused me when I asked, but I was new on the big side, so I felt uncomfortable going alone. Laura sensed that I didn't want to go alone, so she sent Emma to go to the bathroom with me.

Emma escorted me to the bathroom and, as we walked, I noticed something in her hair. She had a small, pink, Hello Kitty bow in her hair that I admired.

We got to the bathroom, and Emma and I went in. When we came out of the bathroom, we walked back to the classroom, and I then went to my cubby to get my workbooks. I worked until snack.

After snack, I went to my classroom, and Laura taught us science. She taught us about a sea animal that lived millions of years ago, and she said, "This animal was called a Eurypterid."

She showed us an illustration of a eurypterid, and she laid out different colored pens to draw with. I went to the light table with pens, a blank piece of paper to draw on, and another piece of paper to copy the information from. Celes was there also, and, as I drew with the pens, I was saying aloud to myself, "Eurypterid, eurypterid, eurypterid." Celes asked me, "Why are you saying 'eurypterid' a lot?"

I didn't answer, but if I could communicate better, I probably would have said to Celes, "Because it's fun and the word 'eurypterid' sounds silly!" We could have laughed and said the silly-sounding word together.

~*~

After class, I had lunch. After I ate, I played alone. After I played, the bell rang, and I ran past the stone bench where I had played with the yellow flower during PE. The flower was wilted now, not pretty like before.

I got to class, and Laura called everyone to the circle. She had a chapter book on the table next to her. She began to read about how two second-grade girls, Ivy and Bean, were trying to get a ghost out of the girls' bathroom by flushing a hair clip, a fossil, and a half-dollar down the toilet as presents for the ghost.

Laura showed us an illustration of the gifts for the ghost, and I started to cry. I left the classroom and went to the lunch tables outside. Emma and Maddyson came out with me, and they tried to comfort me. I started to feel better, and Laura came out of the classroom.

Laura asked Emma and Maddyson, "What happened?"

Emma said, "I think she got scared of the ghost."

But I wasn't scared of the ghost, I thought. *I was scared because Bean flushed the hair clip down the toilet.* If I didn't have autism, I may have said, "It's not the ghost that's scary, I'm scared because Bean flushed Zuzu's hair clip down the toilet!"

Of course, if I didn't have autism, I probably would have been scared because there was a ghost in the bathroom and not because the girl's hair clip got flushed down the toilet.

As a girl with autism, I didn't like things to disappear; I liked knowing that things were safe and I

68

got scared when I thought things might be gone forever. I screamed and cried if a marble rolled under the couch or a toy fell in the pool. That's why it scared me when Ivy and Bean flushed the girl's hair clip down the toilet. But that probably wouldn't have made sense to anyone else.

~*~

On Friday, at the end of my first week in Laura's class, I did all my classes and spent my recess times playing alone and watching other kids play. At the end of the day, Mom came to pick me up. She talked with Laura, and she read my work chart for the week.

Mom read out loud, "Being careless... Being careless... Throwing tantrums!?"

Mom was confused after reading my work chart, but Laura explained that *Being Careless* and *Throwing Tantrums* were just the names of books, and that I wasn't actually being careless or throwing tantrums. Finally, Mom and Laura finished their conversation, and Mom drove me home.

I didn't like my first week of school on the big

side because I still felt like a little girl instead of a big girl. Almost everyone in my class was six years old or older, and I thought I was the only person who was five years old.

I missed the little side, so I snuck onto the little side one day at recess. When I got there, Courtney was celebrating her birthday by eating cake. Her mom had come to school to give pieces of chocolate cake to Courtney's classmates. She thought I was just another student in Maria's class, so she gave me a piece of delicious cake.

If I didn't have autism, I probably would have bragged to the kids on the big side that I got cake from Courtney's mom and that they didn't. Many kids my age would usually brag if they got cake when everyone else didn't, but that wasn't really my personality.

Chapter 10

My Earthquake Kit

It was finally the last day of school. After my first week on the big side, things got more familiar, and I finally felt like I belonged there. I still didn't have any close friends, but every now and then I'd play with a small group.

All the desks were cleaned up, the cubbies and take-home files were cleaned out, and there were no classes to go to. Instead, there was nothing but playtime!

Mom and Dad had packed me a swimsuit and towel so that I could go on the water slide. It was a tradition on the big side, on the last day of school, for the school to rent an inflatable water slide for the big kids to slide on. The middle-school class went, the upper-elementary school class was next, and finally, my class was allowed to go.

Everyone took turns going down the slide and, when my turn finally came, I climbed up the steps, and I went to the slide. I slid down into the shallow water, and I got back in line so I could go again.

I played on the water slide until the end of the day, and then I dried off and got dressed. When it was time to go, I grabbed my things and got into Dad's truck.

I looked in my cloth take-home bag with all of my school things in it. There was something inside that caught my eye. My earthquake kit! I hadn't seen it since the previous school year!

I took out my earthquake kit and saw my emergency food tightly packed in a Ziploc bag. I saw Pixy Stix of different colors, a small container of Jif peanut butter, a water bottle, and some other items.

I opened a Pixy Stix and poured the sugary powder into my mouth. Delicious! I then dug into the Jif peanut butter. I had missed these things so much!

When I was four, Mom and Dad had packed me an earthquake kit to keep at school. It was packed with different foods and items in case an earthquake occured. I had thought that the earthquake kit was mine to take home and to take to school whenever I wanted.

The day I took it to school, I had wanted to take it home at the end of the day. That day, when Dad and I were walking to his truck so he could take me home, I suddenly remembered my earthquake kit. *I forgot my earthquake kit!* I thought. I said to Dad, "Earthquake kit!"

Dad had laughed as he said, "There's no earthquake!" If I was able to communicate better, I might have said, "But I need my earthquake kit! It's in the classroom!"

Dad would have said, "The earthquake kit is packed for emergencies, not for regular snacking."

I thought that I wasn't supposed to leave my earthquake kit at school, and that the food was for me to eat whenever I wanted, so I was very upset to leave it at school, but no one understood that.

Chapter 11

Wooj

Wooj. What a strange-sounding word. Wooj was the name of my imaginary friend when I was little. He was a fourteen-year-old boy from Oakland, California, and he bullied people who were mean to me. He had pale skin and light brown hair. I would take him to my school, and I would play with him on the playground. Other kids probably thought it was weird that I played with my imaginary friend on the playground at school, but I didn't care.

Here is the origin of Wooj. When I was four, I was playing on Mom's phone and made a new contact. I typed "wooj" in the name box. Mom smiled and asked me, "Who's Wooj? Is he your imaginary friend?"

An idea sparked in my head. "Yes," I answered. That is how I got the idea of having an imaginary friend named Wooj.

~*~

When I was six, and in my second year in Laura's class, I decided to take Wooj to school. Wooj and I got to class, and we sat at my desk. I had a piece of paper on my desk that said, "Saved for Wooj." I think Laura became a bit concerned about my obsession with Wooj and thought it was impeding my ability to socialize.

At recess, I was hanging on the play structure and playing with Wooj. I felt that Wooj and I were close friends, and that we could play together and have lots of fun. I didn't know that this was going to change.

When I got back to class, Laura told me, "You can't bring Wooj to school anymore."

I wondered why, but I didn't ask. I didn't actually follow Laura's directions, but I also didn't know why she didn't like Wooj. Was he not good enough? Did he distract me from work? Why? Did Laura actually mean what she said?

A few days later, on Picture Day, I decided that I was going to take Wooj with me for my school picture to be taken. I took Wooj to school (as usual), went to class, and then I exclaimed, "I can't wait for Wooj to be in my school picture!"

Laura was probably right next to me when I spoke, and she got pretty annoyed at me.

"I told you that you're not allowed to bring Wooj to school. He has to stay at home," Laura said.

She was mad at me! What was I going to do? I'd have to leave my imaginary friend at home! Who would I play with?

Dad was there with me the whole time. He said, "You're gonna have to only see Wooj at home."

I couldn't bear to not have Wooj by my side. There would be so much empty space at my desk without him! How could Laura do this?

I understand now why Laura wouldn't let me bring Wooj to school. She was concerned that bringing Wooj to school could distract me in class, and that people would think that it was strange that I was playing and talking to an imaginary friend. I didn't understand why I couldn't bring Wooj to school when I was six, but as I learned more about autism, I could look back and realize how other people might see me.

I felt that Wooj and I were close friends and that
we could play together and have lots of fun.

Chapter 12

Rodent Picnics

One day, when I was six years old, Dad decided to take me to Smart and Final. We needed to get muffins for Mom's teacher training meeting. I didn't know about the meeting until Dad and I got back from Smart and Final with muffins. We went to Pop-Pop's garage, which he calls his man cave, where Mom would be holding her training workshops for the week.

I went into Pop-Pop's man cave with Dad, and I saw that the room had a couple tables with a row of learning materials. We gave Mom her muffins; there were banana-nut muffins, blueberry muffins, and chocolate chip muffins. I said hello to the people there that I knew, and I met a couple of new teachers.

Since Mom's meeting was just plain boring to me, I left. I played by myself for the rest of the day.

~*~

The next day, Mom hosted another meeting. Mom was going to host the meetings for a week, and she was already on her second day.

I watched Mom's meeting for barely a minute, but it was quite dull to me, not something a six-year-old girl would find interesting.

I then said, "Tomorrow, you're gonna find a mess in the room and me asleep on the table. You're gonna say, 'Was there a rodent in here?' But it's gonna be me on the table!" The adults paid no heed, and I left.

~*~

That night, I got into my nightgown and brushed my teeth. I grabbed a basket with a couple of dolls, a pillow, a blanket, and my favorite stuffed animal. I came out of the house through the screen door, and I went to Pop-Pop's man cave and decided to make a mess.

I dumped cubes on the table. Some spilled on the floor. Perfect! I dumped learning tiles out of the box. There were now tiny squares on the table and floor. I made more of a mess. After making a huge mess, I was kind of hungry. I had already eaten dinner, but I wanted a muffin. I took a blueberry muffin out of a box and ate half of it. It was one and a half times the size of a regular muffin, almost as big as a softball.

I got on the table with my blanket and played around with my things. I took another bite of my muffin and laid down to go to sleep. I thought of how the adults were going to react. I imagined them thinking that there had been a rodent in their meeting area the night before. I couldn't wait! I tried to fall asleep but was unsuccessful.

Several minutes later, Mom came into the man cave to do something. She found a huge mess, a half-eaten muffin, and me on the table wrapped in a blanket.

She was annoyed that I had made a huge mess, but she cleaned it up anyway. She put the cubes and the tiles away, she took my muffin off of the table, and she sent me back to the house.

If I didn't have autism, I might have said, "But Mom, I was going to have a rodent picnic! You ruined it!" Maybe I would have just stayed on the table and pretended I was asleep.

I never got to have the complete rodent picnic, as I had planned, but the part I was able to do was fun.

Years later, when I told Mom this story, she thought it was hilarious! She did not remember it at all. She asked me, "Where was I when you did all this?" and I told her, "In the house."

Mom and Dad never understood what rodent picnics were, and I didn't have anyone who liked having rodent picnics with me until months later. That person was my cousin, Jacob.

Jacob came to visit with Aunt Zoe every summer, and Jacob and I would play together. Jacob and Aunt Zoe would stay for a few weeks, and they would leave by the end of the summer.

This particular summer, we had no camps, no commitments, and our imaginations could go wild. On the day he arrived, when Jacob came into my house, I asked him, "Wanna have a rodent picnic?"

He said, "Sure!" He ran back to the guest cottage where Aunt Zoe was unpacking their stuff.

A few minutes later, Jacob came running back to my house with a plastic scepter in his hand and a cape on his back. "I'm ready for the rodent picnic," he announced.

I grabbed a green picnic blanket from the linen closet and took it into Mom and Dad's room. I spread the blanket so that Jacob and I could sit on it. Jacob and I got some snacks and ate them on the blanket. It was our first rodent picnic! We had many more over the summer.

Now that I look back, I realize that I was very lucky to have the experiences that I had with Jacob. Jacob liked anything that had to do with imagination, so he was a good companion for me. He accepted me as I was and was happy to go along with whatever crazy things I wanted to do. He had a lot of crazy ideas of his own as well, which were always fun. He is an amazing cousin, and I loved playing with him.

*I imagined them thinking that there had been a rodent
in their meeting area the night before.*

Chapter 13

Sword Fighting!

Boxes were *everywhere* in Mom's office! Mom had quit her job at a private school and she was going to start her own learning clinic. It was moving day!

Jacob and I were with Mom in her office, bored out of our skulls. I then looked in a drawer and saw two metal rods. I got an idea.

I exclaimed to Jacob, "Let's sword-fight!"

I gave Jacob a "sword," and we began fighting. I heard the impact of our swords echo throughout the room. The sound of them hitting reminded me of fairy-tale movies I had seen.

Mom finally ended our game with, "Let's go."

"Awww," we groaned.

Jacob and I gave our swords to Mom, and we got in her car. Mom then drove us away from the old office.

~*~

We parked in a parking lot by a big building. Mom turned off the car, and we all got out. We went through a door and looked around the new office suite. Cool! It was way bigger than the old office!

I opened another door and saw another room. Jacob and I found two more rooms, but they were all empty. We soon got bored.

Mom was getting more things out of the car. I saw some binding spirals in a box and got an idea. I got a plastic binding spiral for Jacob and one for myself. We went into a room and started sword-fighting with our new "swords."

"Yah!" I shouted.

Jacob blocked my hit with his sword and swung back. "Yah!" he shouted.

We fought more and more until Mom stormed into the room. Mom took back her binding spirals, which were now bent. Jacob and I could tell from her face that she was mad. When everything was unpacked from the car, Mom drove us back home.

~*~

Later that day, Mom got a call from the owner of the new office building. He said that he had gotten a noise complaint from one of the neighboring offices, and, because of that, Mom gave me a lecture.

Mom lectured me about how Jacob and I were shouting, and she said that people from the neighboring offices were disrupted from their work. Mom never punished me for this, but it was punishment enough to listen to her lecture.

Chapter 14

Simon

At Montessori, I didn't play with many people until a boy named Simon came to school. I was six and he was five when he arrived at the beginning of my third year in Laura's class.

Simon had blonde-brown hair down to his shoulders and pale skin, and he was the nicest school friend I had. I know now that, like me, he was perceived as odd by other kids. He sometimes made weird noises, and he was obsessed with cats and planes.

On his first day at school, we played cats and climbed around my favorite tall play structure in the sand. It had a pole and bars all put together to look like a tower.

Simon said, "I'm gonna be a girl cat and pretend I laid eggs." Then he went to the bottom of the play structure and pretended to protect his "eggs."

Talise was sitting on the play structure we were at, and she overheard our conversation. She said to Simon, "You're a *boy*, and cats *don't* lay eggs!" Then Talise walked off to play somewhere else.

Simon looked offended, but we ignored Talise's comment and went back to playing cats together.

After that, I didn't hang out with Talise much anymore. Instead, I considered Simon as a best friend. Talise wasn't really a friend, now that I think about it.

Simon was going through a phase where he was obsessed with cats. Simon loved cats, and he and I would play cat games every day at school. I wanted to have a boyfriend and, in my opinion, Simon was *perfect* for a boyfriend. We both loved cats, we were in the same class, and we were close friends.

Outside, one of the teachers, Kimmy, was telling a story about this bratty boy named Billy who she had made up. Most of the kids from the lower and upper-elementary classrooms were either on the swings or on a little dome-ish structure listening to Kimmy tell us about Billy.

Kimmy had reddish-brown hair and pale skin, and she was the funniest teacher at the school. She told such funny stories; even the middle schoolers listened to her Billy stories. Kimmy would listen to our ideas and incorporate them into her stories, which all of the kids loved!

When she was in the middle of telling a story about Billy driving his mom's car, Simon fell off the dome-ish play structure and hit his nose on one of the metal bars. I thought, *My boyfriend!*

Simon was never really my boyfriend, and I didn't know what a "boyfriend" really meant. I just thought that it meant a boy who you will marry in the future. That made sense in my philosophy.

I came home that day saying to Mom, "I have a boyfriend."

Mom said, "What's his name?"

I said, "Simon."

"Does he *know* he's your boyfriend?"

"Nope." I said.

Then Mom talked to me about what a boyfriend meant and the difference between a boyfriend and a crush. So, I decided that I had a crush on Simon and that he was not my boyfriend.

A couple weeks later, Simon said to me, "I want to marry you."

"So, we're boyfriend and girlfriend, right?" I asked.

Little did I know that Simon's and my relationship was just puppy love. We did not have a real boyfriend-girlfriend relationship, but we had lots of fun together.

~*~

One day, I showed Simon the honeysuckle shrub growing on the fence that created a border separating the big side from the little side. I also taught him that honeysuckle flowers have nectar on the inside. I showed Simon that you have to remove the green bottom of the honeysuckle to get the nectar out of the flower.

The flowers grew in various shades of yellow and white, so it was hard to tell which flowers had nectar and which flowers didn't. Simon would call the honeysuckle "honeysuckers," and I would tell him *dozens* of times, "They aren't honeysuckers, they're honeysuckles!"

Later that school year, by the time I was seven and Simon was six, I had acquired three friends at school. I had Simon, and I had made friends with Courtney, who had moved up to the big side, and a boy named Ezekiel.

Ezekiel and Courtney were both six, like Simon. Ezekiel liked cats, just like Simon and me. But, unlike the boys, Courtney and I weren't *obsessed* with cats.

We all liked to hang out together and, during music class, we would all sit together. Laura made a rule that kids had to sit in a circle in a boy-girl pattern. This pattern was probably made so that best friends couldn't sit next to and distract each other during class. Luckily, I had friends that were boys, so the boy-girl pattern didn't affect my cat-playing group. We were following the rules, and Laura couldn't separate us. She never tried to separate us, but, if Simon and I distracted each other, I never noticed.

Other times, Simon and I would play together,

just him and me. We would also just talk sometimes.

As I mentioned before, Simon and I loved to play cats. We would play pretend games like Sea Cats, regular Cats, and a favorite of ours, Snow Cats.

Lots of kids liked to poke fun at us for playing Snow Cats. Richard always commented on Simon's obsession with cats, and so did Kaiden.

One day at PE, Richard yelled at Simon and me, "Snow Cats suck!"

Kaiden then yelled, "Yeah, Snow Cats suck!"

I ignored their comments, but Simon got angry and yelled at them. I didn't say anything to Richard and Kaiden, but if I were more assertive, I'd probably have said to them something like, "Shut your big blubbers! If you make fun of us, you'll go home with fat lips!"

After Richard and Kaiden had made fun of Simon and me many times, Laura lectured everyone in our classroom about making fun of Snow Cats. I was glad she did that because Richard and Kaiden stopped making fun of Simon and me after that.

~*~

At home, I watched the movie *Barbie: A*

Fashion Fairytale, which is a movie where Barbie mistakenly believes that her boyfriend broke up with her over the phone.

At school, I asked Simon, "What if we break up someday?"

Simon said, "We will never break up."

I agreed. We would never break up.

I had so much fun in Laura's class with Simon, Ezekiel, and Courtney. I felt like I was lucky to finally have such an amazing year in Laura's class with my friends who loved cats.

I had been allowed an extra year in the lower-elementary classroom because, even though I knew all of the academic stuff and could read chapter books before most of my classmates could, Mom and Dad decided that I still needed to learn how to play pretend games with other kids.

I'm glad I had that time, but I didn't know that my friendship with Simon, Courtney, and Ezekiel was going to change someday.

After that, I didn't hang out with Talise much anymore.
Instead, I considered Simon as a best friend.

Chapter 15

A Playdate

As a child with autism, I didn't know how to tell my friends that I wanted to have playdates with them. I also didn't know how to tell my parents that I wanted to have a playdate with Simon.

Mom and Simon's mom, Aliza, crossed paths one day, and they had a conversation together. They talked to each other about Simon and me having a playdate sometime soon, and they exchanged phone numbers. Then they found Simon and me together, playing by the honeysuckle bush.

Aliza told Simon, "Time to go."

Simon said, "I don't want to go!"

"And it's time for us to go too, Mickie," Mom said. When I was six, I changed the spelling of my nickname from "Mickey" to "Mickie," with a heart over each "i."

I said to Simon, "Bye, Simon! See you tomorrow!"

"Bye!" Simon yelled to me.

Mom took me to the school parking lot, and we walked to her car. We opened the doors, got in, buckled our seat belts, and she drove us home.

On the ride home, Mom said to me, "You and Simon are going to have a playdate tomorrow. After school, Simon's mom, Aliza, will pick you up from school and drive you to their house!"

I said, "I can't wait to go to Simon's house! It has a million stories!"

Mom was confused. She said, "Simon's house only has one story. Don't you remember it from Halloween? We trick-or-treated at his house."

"But he has a million stories at his house," I told Mom. "Simon told me that when I asked him."

Mom answered, "He probably thought that you meant storybooks."

Now that makes more sense, I thought.

~*~

The next day, Dad dropped me off at school,

and he walked with me to my classroom. He gave me a hug and a kiss and then walked away down the hall as I opened the classroom door.

I went to my cubby so I could grab my workbooks, journal, and the book I was reading, and then I did my work.

Later, I went to art class and did art until snack break. I ate my snack with Simon, and then we went to the honeysuckle shrub, and we played Cats until Laura rang the bell for the lower-elementary kids to come to class.

Back in class, I did more work. After Laura let us out of class for lunch break, all of the hot-lunch kids ran to the lunch line. When it was my turn, the lunch lady put the main food item on my plate, and then I asked for the side items I liked.

After I ordered my favorite side items, I took a spork from a bin and went to a lunch table where Simon was sitting. We started eating together.

We finished eating, and then we played with Ezekiel and Courtney. When the bell rang, we went back to class.

~*~

Back in class, Laura taught us science, the subject I liked the most. It was a subject I liked because most of the things we did were hands-on, not just from books and lectures.

We would do activities like touch the different rocks and minerals that Laura showed us, paint watercolor pictures of prehistoric animals we had learned about, paint fossil replicas with colors we liked, color and draw things we had learned about, and other cool projects like that.

Laura finished teaching us science, and she then dismissed school. Finally, it was time for my playdate with Simon!

Aliza came to pick Simon and me up, and we got in her car and drove away from school. She parked her car in front of a store and got out. She told Simon and me to stay in the car, and she left for a few minutes.

She came back to the car with two large, chocolate-chip cookies, one for me and one for Simon. Aliza gave us our cookies, and Simon and I thanked her. We ate our cookies as Aliza drove us to Simon's house.

We got to Simon's house and Aliza let us in. Aliza offered us almond milk. Since Simon was allergic to dairy, his family didn't have regular milk. Aliza poured Simon and me each a glass of almond milk, and we drank it happily.

After Simon and I drank our almond milk, he showed me his room. He opened the door and I looked around. He had a couple bookshelves with books, a bed shaped like a car, a rug, and some stuffed animals. He showed me his black and white stuffed cat that he slept with, named Spunky, and I told him about how I slept with my stuffed cat, Sagwa. We then went outside to his backyard to play.

His backyard had lots of shade and a play structure to play on. We climbed his play structure, and we talked until Dad picked me up. I said goodbye to Simon and Aliza, and Dad took me home in his truck.

My day had been so fun! I had a playdate, I got a cookie, and I tried almond milk. It was great!

Chapter 16

My Journal

In the lower-elementary classroom, the kids had journals to write in. I wrote a lot in my school journal when I was six and seven, and writing came to be easy for me. But Mom, and sometimes Dad, always seemed to be my enemy in my school journal.

I also always seemed to share my family business, so if Mom was annoyed at me for putting the toothpaste in the toothbrush holder, I would write in my journal that I was really mad at Mom for taking the toothpaste out of the toothbrush holder. Sometimes Laura thought that I was mad at Mom, but I loved Mom. I just got annoyed with her easily. Here are two of my entries:

Mickie (no date in journal)

One day I said I was going to live in my playhouse but I do not live in it right now. I said that on Sunday I was supposed to go to church. I miss church. I was going to pack my things like my dolls, my dollhouse where Jim and Max and their sisters, my unicorns, my toy animals, my house jewelry box, my cereals I was going to buy a sink and a toddler thing and a refriderator and a towel and I was going to get my clothes and my laundry basket and I was going to wear any clothes to public like my Rapunzel dress, my Tinkerbell dress, my Aurora dress, my chinese sweater, Tinkerbell shoes, Tinkerbell wings, my Merida dress, my Merida wig, my Tiana dress, and my Snow white dress.

Mickie 3-28-13

While my dad is at home I will buy some Cheetos and while we are in the plane I ~~wite~~ will get out the Cheetos and eat them. My mom and dad will say where did you get Cheetos? I would say "Secret."

In my perspective, there was nothing wrong with my entries. I felt that I was just writing in my journal about my daily life.

The first journal entry was about my planning to run away from home and move to my playhouse. I wanted to move to my playhouse because Mom wouldn't take me to the church around the corner from our house.

I liked the idea of going to church a lot, so I wanted to go every Sunday. Mom was not a big fan of church, but I went to church two times with Dad before he decided not to take me anymore. Mom and Dad didn't like the fear method this church used to teach kids about Christianity, and they didn't want my brain bloating up with bad information.

I was really mad at Mom for not letting me go to church, so I stormed to my room and put a sign on my door. It said in all capitals, "LET ME GO TO CHURCH NOW!"

I sulked in my room, and I then got an idea. My idea was to run away from home and live in the playhouse. If I ran away from home, I could wear costumes in public, even if it wasn't Halloween yet. I could eat whatever I wanted. By then I shared a room with my baby sister, Daisy. But, if I ran away, I could have my own room! I could even wear my "Chinese sweater."

My "sweater" wasn't really a sweater. It was made in China, but it wasn't really Chinese. Mom would get annoyed when I wore it in public. She told me not to, but sometimes I wore it anyway. Mom said it was a "cheap" shirt and only for costumes. It had some holes in it too.

I didn't really work out the details of living alone though. I didn't have enough money to buy food. The playhouse didn't have water, a sink, a refrigerator, or a toilet! How would I get clean? How would I get to school? Would I get in trouble with Mom and Dad? How would all of my things fit into the playhouse? I'd break the doorway trying to fit my bed into the playhouse!

If I had thought more about it, I would have planned to move into the guest cottage. It has more room, a bathroom, a kitchen with a sink and a refrigerator, a table that can fit two people, a TV, a couch, a chair, a king-sized bed, soap, shampoo and conditioner, a heater, an air conditioner, electricity, and plumbing. I wish I had thought of all this at the time!

For moving to my playhouse, I wanted to pack my dollhouse where my Legos (Jim, Max, and their sisters) lived. I wanted to have a potty chair in my playhouse, but, to be polite, I wrote "toddler thing" in my journal instead of "potty chair." I knew that my teacher was going to read my journal.

The second journal entry is about planning to sneak Cheetos on the plane when I went for a family trip to Alabama, where my dad's side of the family lives.

Dad didn't want me to eat Cheetos because they aren't healthy, and they have a bunch of chemicals that I don't need in my body.

Dad would never buy the cereals that many families would keep in their pantries for their kids to have for breakfast. Cereals like Frosted Flakes, Cocoa Puffs, Froot Loops, Reese's Puffs, Cinnamon Toast Crunch, Apple Jacks, and Lucky Charms would remain on the store shelves when Dad and I shopped for my cereal.

Instead of the sugary cereals, Dad would get me "O Organics" cereals, and I'd get jealous, and annoyed at Dad, when I'd see other people's shopping carts with Cinnamon Toast Crunch boxes in them.

Parents would send their kids to school with Pop Tarts, Cheetos, Danimals drinks, Go-gurts, Oreos, and other stuff like that. Instead of these treats, I was sent to school with rice cakes and peanut butter. These were tasty, but I would see some of my classmates eating their brightly-colored Foot Rolls and others munching on Oreos while I, and a few other kids, ate healthy snacks.

I seldom got junk food; the only time I would get junk food was when Jacob came to visit with Aunt Zoe.

Aunt Zoe would get Jacob a bunch of snacks that I would ask for whenever they were visiting. It wasn't every day that I would get Foot Rolls. Snacks that I had never even heard of were given to Jacob by Aunt Zoe. When they visited each summer, I would get

Go-gurts, Danimals, Foot Rolls, Scooby Doo gummy characters, Kraft macaroni and cheese, Lucky Charms, Froot Loops, and Cinnamon Toast Crunch. It was awesome!

Mom, and sometimes Dad, always seemed
to be my enemy in my school journal.

Chapter 17

Change

When I was almost eight, I finally transferred to Ruth's class, which was the upper-elementary classroom.

On my first day of school in my new classroom, I noticed lots of differences between the upper-elementary classroom and the lower-elementary classroom.

In my new classroom, we got to make ourselves tea and snacks and have them in class! Also, there were different jobs for different kids every week. One kid would be the Water Bearer, and that kid would fill the water pitcher in the kitchen and bring it back to the classroom. Another kid would sweep the hallways. Other kids would do other jobs.

We also got to use desktop computers for educational apps! In the upper-elementary classroom, we got to use actual dishes and mugs instead of having our snacks on paper towels, and we got to pour hot water out of a kettle to make our own tea!

We were limited to one sugar cube, at the most, for tea, and I followed that rule pretty well. I was still close friends with Simon, but he was still in the lower-elementary classroom.

On the first day of school in my new class, I realized that, not only were we in different classrooms, Simon and I also had different class schedules. This meant that I had nobody to play with at snack recess.

There were a few kids I didn't like in Ruth's class, like Alana and Noah. Noah was annoying and rude, so I disliked him. Alana was a bully to me in preschool and kindergarten, so I did not like her at all.

Mom observed me in my new class, and she realized that Simon and I had different snack recess schedules. I didn't want to play with anyone but Simon because he was my "boyfriend."

Because making friends and playing with other kids was so challenging for me, Mom and my teacher agreed that I could have more recess time to play with my friends from the lower-elementary classroom, Simon, Courtney, and Ezekiel.

My new teacher, Ruth, had blonde hair that was always put in a bun. She had pale skin and she was really nice. I mostly liked my first semester in the upper-elementary classroom.

In addition to all the other cool new stuff, we did this great activity called Timez Attack. This is a fun, educational, computer game where you pass awesome levels by solving math problems. So many kids in the class loved it.

In Ruth's class, I was also obsessed with reading; I'd read for long periods of time and lose track of my work because I didn't know how to manage my time. I'd just let time fly by reading books in the classroom.

Right before we went on winter break for Christmas and New Year's, I began having problems with Simon. Once, I asked Simon if I could play with him in the play house, and his response was, "There's no more room."

I thought something close to, *He's my boyfriend*

and I'm his girlfriend. How could he do this? Situations like this had been going on for a while now, and I got more and more annoyed with Simon.

During winter break, I told Mom, "Simon dumped me!"

Mom said, "How did he dump you?"

I said, "When I ask if I can play with Simon in the little play house, he always says, 'There's no more room.'"

Mom said, "He didn't dump you, but it sounds like you might have to dump him," or something like that.

That sparked an idea in my head.

One day at lunch, after winter break, Simon sat next to me. He said, "I have apple slices. They're organic."

I said, "Cool!" We both loved when foods were organic.

Simon asked me, "Do you want to play Cats with Ezekiel, Courtney, and me?"

"Sure!"

I ate my lunch and showed the teacher my plate.

She said that I could play, and I ran to the wooden play house. When I got there, Simon had already started a game with Courtney and Ezekiel.

I asked, "Can I play?"

Simon said, "There's no more room."

It was time for me to take the bull by the horns and break up with Simon.

I said, "Fine! I'm breaking up with you!" and stomped off angrily.

After that incident, I would try to get Simon's attention. For example, if Simon was on the swings, I would try to get his attention by swinging two or more swings away from him and acting as if I were better than him and pretending that I was better off without him. I was mad at him, but I really missed him. I missed our talks, our trike rides, and our games together.

With the big gap in my social life where my friendship with Simon used to be, I felt very alone. I had nobody else I wanted to play with at school.

There are lots of challenges I had due to ADHD and autism. At eight, I talked a lot more than I did when

I was four, but I still wasn't a very social person.

With ADHD causing problems, I was doing weird things in class like rolling on the rug in my classroom and saying, "I'm doomed! I'm double doomed!" which is a line from a book I liked called *Ivy and Bean Take Care of the Babysitter*, by Annie Barrows.

I don't think anyone knew what I was talking about, so they probably thought that I was not a good person to hang out with, especially when I was rolling on the rug during work time. I saw no problem with how I behaved at the time, but I think my teacher was probably annoyed by my rolling on the rug in the middle of class.

Mom and Dad got me a prescription medication to help me focus better, because incidents like that happened often. They called it my "brain medicine." My brain medicine tasted disgusting; it had a weird sweet flavor that I hated.

To make matters worse, kids at Montessori had to show their plates to the teacher at the lunch tables and ask, "Can I be done?" Because of my medicine, I had no appetite at lunch. I had to eat when I was not hungry.

I tried to convince Mom and Dad to let me stop taking my "brain medicine" because I didn't have an appetite at lunch, and the teachers wouldn't let me go play if I didn't eat all of my lunch. Mom and Dad said they would talk to my teachers, which helped, but, from then on, I would call my medicine Sour Barf Pit, even though there was nothing sour about my medicine.

I think my teacher was probably annoyed by my
rolling on the rug in the middle of class.

Chapter 18

Friends and Foes

In Ruth's class, I made a new friend. I didn't like Noah at first. Then I realized- he liked Minecraft and I liked Minecraft. We could be friends.

Minecraft is this video game you can get on a laptop, a desktop, an X-Box, an iPad, an iPod, an iPhone, or a tablet. You can play Minecraft in two different modes. In creative mode, you can build cool things and fly. In survival mode, you can't fly, and you can turn monsters on and off.

I often played in survival mode without monsters, and Noah always gave me tips on Minecraft. Unfortunately, I was only allowed to play Minecraft on the weekends. I just had to either try to remember the tips Noah gave me until the weekend came, or write his tips down.

Usually, Noah and I chatted about Minecraft by

the yurt, where we did music class once a week.

Noah and I didn't always talk about Minecraft. We also talked about nutrition. This was during my nutrition phase when I was opposed to everything non-organic.

During this phase, I would check all of the ingredients in foods before eating them. Mom would get embarrassed when I looked at the back of cereal cartons at a family member's house in order to see if the cereal had any artificial ingredients.

Noah always said that McDonald's used chicken butts in their burgers, McFlurries, and french fries. I never believed him when he said that.

I had a "nutrition journal" which had a list of all the people at school who didn't eat healthy snacks. I made up kind ways to get the kids who didn't eat healthy foods to eat more healthy, but my methods didn't work.

Kind ways to show people to eat healthy that I made up and wrote in my journal (that don't work):

1. Eat healthy bars in front of them.
2. Eat healthy stuff in front of them.

117

~*~

There was one boy in my class, named Aiden, who had dirty-blonde curls down to his shoulders. Aiden was chubby and ate a lot of junk food, from what I could tell.

One day, at snack time, I was hoping to try to get Aiden to eat healthy. I decided to eat an Odwalla bar across from him at the lunch table and look him in the eye. He didn't get my cue. I took another bite of my bar, even more desperate.

"Why are you staring at me?" Aiden questioned. I finally gave up. He wasn't getting what I was trying to do!

In my brain, I was doing something good for Aiden. If I didn't have autism, I probably wouldn't have cared about what Aiden ate or had such a strange way of trying to change it.

In one of my nutrition journals, I drew a magnifying glass and wrote about "bad" eaters. Some of the people on that list were Aiden, Courtney, Ezekiel, and Melanie. I think Noah would have liked my nutrition journal.

118

I hung out with Noah a lot that year, and I started to develop a crush on him. He was eleven and I was eight, so I was a bit too young to date Noah.

I had a crush on Noah until he started gossiping about Aiden. Aiden was absent one day so, to Noah, it was a perfect day to gossip about him. We sat by the yurt that day and talked.

Noah said, "Aiden smells so bad because he never takes a shower."

I felt compelled to converse, so I said, "Does he even get a haircut?"

"Rarely," Noah answered.

"When Aiden got his first iPod, he dropped it." Noah said. He also made a comment about Aiden's family being poor.

After school, I told Mom and Dad about this, and I wrote down all of the things Noah had said about Aiden. Dad got upset and mentioned these things to Ruth.

After that, I decided to scribble out the things I had written about Aiden in my "nutrition journals" and diaries because I felt bad for Aiden. Even now, I'm embarrassed that I ever judged and gossiped about him.

~*~

Melanie was another kid in Ruth's class, and she was different from Noah. I was okay with her at first, but then she got more and more bossy.

Melanie was someone I would try to avoid. I would write in my diary that she was snooty, and that she would act like she was the boss of me 6/5 (six hours a day, five days a week). To make matters worse, Melanie's desk was near mine, so I had to work near her every day. My class was not really big enough for me to avoid her.

There were fourteen kids in my class, including Melanie and me. I wish I could have been able to just ignore Melanie and move through the day without thinking of or talking to her. If I didn't have autism, I probably wouldn't have been so furious about how bossy she was. With autism, I could get really stuck on certain thoughts and ideas, and it was very difficult for me to let things go without holding long grudges.

I liked to express my anger by writing in my diary, and I had lots to write about. I wrote in my diary about how Melanie was rude and bossy. In my diary, I liked to draw, too. I would draw pictures of bad things happening to Melanie. Looking back, it seems a bit disturbing!

At some point, I became friends with Alana, who used to bully me. She and I would complain about Melanie sometimes. Once, Alana dared Noah to spray Melanie in the face with his water bottle.

ALANA: Truth or Dare?
NOAH: Dare.
ALANA: I dare you to spray Melanie in the face with your water bottle.

So, Noah grabbed his water bottle and found Melanie in the hall. He opened his water bottle and sprayed Melanie. I heard Melanie scream and Noah laugh. It was pretty mean, but Alana, Noah, and I found it funny at the time. Noah seemed to like getting on people's nerves and, like me, he disliked Melanie.

I never tried to annoy Melanie, but I liked keeping things from her. Keeping things secret from

Melanie made me feel like I had power over her and that her tyrannical ways couldn't get the best of me.

I read a *Sabrina the Teenage Witch* comic once, and, in it, there was a teenage girl who was a "female leprechaun." In the comic, leprechauns were more powerful than witches whenever they had their gold nearby. I got the idea that I was a female leprechaun, and I kept gold rocks in my backpack so I could use my "powers."

My rocks weren't actually gold. They were spray-painted gold from when my class learned about the Gold Rush and dug in the sand for them. I kept my "gold" in my backpack so I could do "magic." I didn't try to use my powers on Melanie very often, though.

My school days never centered around avoiding Melanie. Instead, I was able to focus on talking and playing with my friends, Noah and Alana.

Chapter 19

End of the School Year

It was the last week of school, and I was excited to start summer vacation. On some school days, there would be about an hour to read, and I was getting into the *Violet Mackerel* series. The books were really good; I would binge-read these books every day.

I was getting better about keeping my desk neat, too. I had a work chart at the time that was designed to help me master skills that other kids could already do. Other kids would have perfectly neat desks, while my workbooks would be falling on the floor because my school work was spread out all over my desk.

At the time, I also had a habit of going to the bathroom a lot. It didn't have anything negative to do with my health, it was just a habit that got annoying to my teacher. Using my work chart, I was doing better at that, also. Another thing on my chart was that I had to have my work timed because I could spend most of class reading, and I needed a limit.

On the day of our last music class, we didn't have a regular class. Instead, there was a party! There was music and there were popsicles, goldfish crackers, ice cream, and other snacks! I danced with my music group until the next group came in for their party.

My group went back to the classroom, happy. Melanie had a goldfish bag in her hand as we walked.

Back in class, I got out my workbooks and started working. Melanie was eating her goldfish crackers, and I realized something. Goldfish have celery seed in them, and I was allergic to celery! Kids at school who were allergic to peanuts sat farther away from the kids who ate peanuts or peanut butter. Maybe I should sit away from Melanie!

At Montessori, we were allowed to work outside, so I grabbed my work and moved outside to the lunch tables. I worked in my algebra book for a few minutes, and it was fun.

I had asked Ruth for an algebra book a week back, and Ruth had given me one. I knew how to do algebra problems, so it was easy for me. I knew that the dot in problems meant to multiply, and I was solving algebra problems long before my classmates.

DING! DING! DING! Melanie was standing by my table, ringing the bell, trying to get me inside.

"But I'm allergic to celery! Your goldfish..." I wanted her to leave me alone so I could work outside, far away from her and her goldfish crackers.

Melanie interrupted, "It doesn't matter!" She kept ringing the bell over my talking.

Ruth came out of the classroom and saw Melanie and me arguing.

I said, "Melanie's ringing the bell over my voice! I'm trying to tell her that her goldfish crackers have celery and that I'm allergic!"

Melanie said innocently, "I'm just trying to get her inside."

Ruth helped us work our problem out. I went into the classroom with Melanie and Ruth and, to my relief, Melanie's goldfish crackers were gone.

~*~

After school, I got into Mom's car. I said to

Mom, "Melanie was bossy to me! I was outside at the lunch tables, working, and Melanie came out and rang the bell right next to me! I tried to tell her that her goldfish has celery and that I'm allergic to celery. She said, 'It doesn't matter!'"

"It *doesn't* matter," Mom said. She seemed confused and annoyed that I was making a big deal about it. I was frustrated at her response.

I said, "But Pete and Quinn sit away from kids eating peanuts." Pete and Quinn were both kids who were severely allergic to peanuts. They couldn't be near peanuts, so they had to sit far away from people who were eating them. The school had to serve sunflower butter to all of the kids instead of peanut butter, and sunflower seeds were an alternative to peanuts.

When we got home, I went into my closet and grabbed my diary. I grabbed a marker and wrote:

Dear Diary,
Today there was a party in the yurt. There was lemonade, applesauce, ice cream, goldfish crackers, chips, popsicles, and other stuff. when we came

back, Melanie Devaux had goldfish crackers on her desk!! Then when Melanie rang the bell, she looked angry!!! I tried to tell her the reason why, but she rang the bell over me! When I told her the reason why I was outside Melanie said "It doesn't matter!"

Mic

6/5/14

Chapter 20

My Summer

In the summer, when Dad needed to work, Daisy and I had to go to daycare at Montessori. Dad took Daisy and me in his truck. When we got there, Dad let us out of his truck. By now, Daisy was one and a half, and she was able to walk.

I never looked forward to daycare. Most of the kids ranged from infants to five-year-olds. I wanted to sleep in and play on my iPad at home, but Mom and Dad both had to work, and I didn't have a say in whether I went to daycare or not.

Daisy and I went over to the little baby wagon that she liked, and one of her classmates, Emily, got in with her. Emily was two years old, and she had short brown hair that she always wore with a hairclip.

I took Emily and Daisy around in the baby wagon, and, as I pulled them, I looked behind me at the toddlers. Daisy took Emily's shoe and tossed it over the side. It landed with a smack on the ground!

I exclaimed, "Daisy!"

Emily looked irritated. I stopped pulling the wagon and grabbed Emily's shoe from the ground. I gave Emily her shoe and helped her put it back on her foot.

SMACK! SMACK! Daisy took both of Emily's shoes and tossed them on the ground. Again, Emily seemed annoyed. I picked Emily's shoes up off of the ground, and I put them back on her feet.

I said to Emily, "If you don't like when Daisy touches you, say, 'Don't touch my body!'" I had learned that in a safety class when I was in preschool. I kept pulling the wagon, and Daisy kept taking Emily's shoes and tossing them over the side.

Emily soon gave up and stopped caring whether or not Daisy threw her shoes, but, whenever Daisy threw Emily's shoes over the side of the wagon, I got embarrassed. If my thinking had been more flexible, I might have thought that Daisy's behavior was funny; I probably wouldn't have been so frustrated with her.

"Snack time!" the teacher yelled.

I ate my snack with everyone, and, when I finished, I put my snack container away on the shelf that held kids' belongings. I went into the daycare room and saw a girl with blonde hair.

I asked her, "What's your name?"

She said, "Ella."

"I'm Mickie."

Ella's name was easy for me to remember. There was a fairy named Ella in one of the *Rainbow Magic* books, which was a series I liked to read.

Ella was four years old and she liked me a lot. Even though I was eight, she was someone I liked to play with. I liked to play with her, Emily, a girl named Belinda, another girl named Lucia, and Alana. Alana was the only one my age, but she didn't come to daycare often.

Lucia was four years old, and she liked playing with me also. Belinda was five. She and I liked to play together and have Dad spray us with the garden hose.

There were usually only younger kids in daycare, so that was part of the reason I mostly played with little kids. Also, as a kid with autism, I preferred the company of younger kids. For me, it was easier to play with younger kids because they played more pretend games that were engaging to me. I felt like I fit in better with them; they looked up to me and accepted me.

For another part of the summer, I did summer camp at Mom's office with my cousin, Jacob, and my classmate, Alana. In summer camp, I did Spanish class, a language arts class, a computer class, and a math class with a boy named Geoff.

Spanish class wasn't loads of fun. I did learn some things, but I felt that the way my teacher taught me wasn't very exciting. We did *Learning to Sequence* stories, which were cards with pictures that were supposed to be put in order. After I put the cards in order, I had to tell the story in Spanish. I learned from this, but I preferred activities that required more creativity.

My teacher once thought that it would be fun for me to do an online Spanish game, but the game was incredibly cheesy and boring to me. The game was designed for preschoolers, and I was eight and a half!

I complained to Mom about how my Spanish teacher wouldn't tell me how to say "spring green" in Spanish. I kept asking her, and I got more and more exasperated when she wouldn't tell me. Mom told me that I had to speak more Spanish when I asked her questions, and this suggestion actually helped me because my teacher was more responsive when I spoke Spanish.

Math was actually very fun. My teacher would play math games with Geoff and me. Working with Geoff was fun, but, at first, I didn't like him much.

One time, in class, I tried to do something with my "leprechaun powers," and I was muttering to myself about using them, trying to get attention. Geoff said to me, "You don't have powers!"

I got mad at him, and I held a grudge against him for a while. But later, Geoff and I started having fun in class. We did an activity that involved place value sometimes, and we would go up to numbers in the quintillions. For some reason, Geoff and I were obsessed with the number two, so a lot of the numbers we used for place value had two in them.

In summer camp, I also did BrainWare Safari, which was a jungle-themed computer game for strengthening processing skills. In this program, you had to solve puzzles and play Tic-Tac-Toe against the computer. There were more games than that, and I completed all of the levels on most of them. A lot of them were easy for me, but I found a few of the levels extremely difficult.

For language arts, I read *Bridge to Terabithia*, by Katherine Patterson, with some classmates. It started out great, but, in the middle of the book, an important character dies. While the teacher was reading about how the character died, I was having a hard time focusing. I was rolling myself into a burrito with the rug, fidgeting with the carpet, and not seeming to pay attention.

Later that day, one of my classmates told my mom that I wasn't paying attention in class, and that I didn't seem to understand that one of the characters had died. I understood that a character had died, I was just feeling restless and fidgety, so I wasn't very focused on the story. Also, when I was younger, I didn't respond to negative emotions much.

Now, people consider me to be very sensitive and empathetic, but it was a long time before I could process negative experiences and emotions in others.

When I was younger, and someone got hurt or was crying, or there was a sad part in a book or movie, I didn't really react. I didn't take perspective well, but it didn't mean that I didn't love or care about people. Empathy just didn't come naturally to me. I had to be taught that other people's feelings were just like my own before I could empathize. If I were to re-read *Bridge to Terabithia* now, I would be crying my eyes out when I got to that part!

When Mom and I were in the car going home, she told me about what the other student had said. I was annoyed because I felt that I understood the book well, and that the student didn't know what she was talking about! But, if I didn't have autism, I probably wouldn't have been rolling myself up in the rug and playing with the carpet during an important and moving part of the book. I probably would have been more attentive to the emotional meaning of the scene.

Even though she used to bully me, Alana was my friend for the summer. I told her that I had a crush on Rafaele. Rafaele was the cutest out of all the boys in the upper-elementary classroom, and he charmed most of the girls in my class. He had light-brown hair, pale skin, and a smile that I liked. I knew that Alana wouldn't tell anyone about my crush...

Alana went to summer camp with me, and she and I played together a few times. She was one of my closest friends at the time; my previous grudge against her had been forgotten.

One day, after summer camp, Mom and I went to drop Alana off at Montessori. At Montessori, I was hoping to say hello to Ella and spend some time with her.

Mom wanted to go straight home after dropping Alana off, but as soon as we got to the gate, I ran to the daycare room to play with Ella. I opened the daycare

135

room door and saw Ella, Lucia, and some other kids.

Lucia said loudly, "Hi, Mickie!"

I quickly tried to shush her. I thought that she was going to give my presence away and my mom would find me.

I whispered, "Hide me!"

I hid behind the toy shelf so Mom couldn't see me. I saw Mom through the daycare window, and I kept quiet.

Even though I was quiet, Mom opened the door. She found me and took me out of the daycare room. I said goodbye to my friends and left with Mom.

I probably should have said goodbye to Alana when she left and, if I wanted to see Ella, I should've just gone in the daycare room really quick and said, "Hi," and then left. But I was very focused on Ella and how I wanted to play with her, and I didn't think it was fair that I had to leave my friend.

The next day, I wrote in my diary about what had happened the day before, but, at the time, I blamed Ella for not hiding me. I wrote:

Dear Diary,

Yesterday Mom came to Montessori to take Alana to my school and I wanted to have some time with Ella. I went into the daycare room to try to sneak time with Ella. Then my mom was coming to the daycare room, and I said to Ella, "Hide me!!! Hide me!!" well, she didn't! Then my mom took me home!

♡

Mickie 6/21/14

Family Photos

Playing dress-up was one of my
favorite childhood activities.

My "Fancy Nancy" outfit.

Goofing off with Daisy's baby hats
was so fun!

I loved pretending that I was
a princess.

My first day of ballet class.

Painting a "Chinese Water Slide."

The Christmas train ride is one of my best
childhood memories.

The first day of first grade,
which is the day I met Simon.

Father's Day family photo!

Visiting Yosemite National Park.

Playing in the snow at Lake Tahoe.

I loved playing chess with Dad. I won most of the time!

Holding Daisy for the first time!

With baby Daisy, my family
was now complete.

Sibling photos for picture day.

My family!

Chapter 21

Friend Trouble

My second year in Ruth's class was mostly fun, but it wasn't fun at all during one part of the day. At recess, I didn't really have anybody to play with.

At lunch on the first day of school, I sat with Courtney, and we ate together. Courtney had her own lunch from home, and I had hot lunch.

We had a conversation and, after we ate lunch, we went on the playground together. We pretended that we were kittens, and that I was the mean big sister.

Alana had gone to a new school, and Noah had moved away, but Courtney had moved up this year. She and I were now in the same class again, which meant that we could play more. Our game ended when someone rang the bell.

The kids all went into the classroom, and Ruth started a game. The game was that each kid had to have a picture of an animal taped to his or her back. Other classmates could give you hints, and you would have to guess what animal you had on your back based on the hints you were given.

This game was really fun, and I was able to tell that I had a white tiger picture on my back based on the hints I was given.

We did some more first-day activities, and we got to choose the Jobs of the Week. I chose to be the Royal Messenger, which is the person who takes important papers and notes to the office.

After this activity, school was dismissed. I went to the playground to play, and Rafaele and his group invited me to play with them. Rafaele's group included his younger brother, Ricardo, a boy named Darren, and other kids including Luke, Ezekiel, Cathy, Kaiden, and Jordan. I knew them all from previous school years, and we all played a game where we pretended to be the animals that had been taped on our backs during the activity in the classroom.

I still had a crush on Rafaele, and so did some other girls at school.

~*~

The next day, during lunch recess, I played with Courtney and another girl named Justice, who was a year or two younger than me. I had known her for a long time.

Courtney took Justice and me to a table under a tree, and she told us about something that she found hilarious. She told us about how she looked up images of naked cartoon characters on her phone (which didn't even have a phone number because she was only seven).

She described the pictures, and we all burst out laughing. She told us that she would bring her phone one day and show us the pictures.

Courtney and Justice wanted us all to kiss one day. That would make us sisters, according to them. They also wanted us to all show each other our private parts, but I didn't really want to do that.

Clearly, they were both pretty childish; not that I wasn't, but they were a bit more immature than I was. They enjoyed games involving private parts, kissing, and being sneaky, which is all pretty normal kid stuff, but I wasn't into those things, so I didn't really go along with it.

Alana came back to Montessori a few days later. We had drifted apart after hanging out at summer camp, but we weren't enemies or anything. Unfortunately, a few days after she came back to school, she told *everyone* in my class, and even some of the middle schoolers, about my huge crush on Rafaele.

One of the middle schoolers, Grace, asked me, "Do you have a crush on Rafaele?"

I said, "Yes."

Grace said, "Alana told me. She told everyone, but I won't tell him."

Grace was nice. She wouldn't tell anyone about my crush, unlike Alana! I was so annoyed at Alana! She had backstabbed me! I wanted to tell everyone that she also had a crush on Rafaele, which she had revealed to me when I told her about my crush on him.

Later that day, after science, I confronted Alana. As we were getting scratch paper from a shelf, I told her, "You shouldn't have told everyone about my crush on Rafaele!"

"It's none of your business!" she retorted.

I ran out of the room to the lunch tables. I sat at one of the lunch tables, crying. Grace knew about my crush on Rafaele, Emma knew, Kaiden knew, Cathy knew, Jordan knew, Darren knew, Ricardo knew, the rest of my class knew, the middle schoolers knew, and, worst of all, Rafaele knew.

As the science teacher, Kristel, was walking out of my classroom, she saw me. She asked me, "Why are you crying? What happened?"

"Alana backstabbed me!" I cried.

Kristel said, "I hate when that happens."

I continued my pity party. Alana wasn't really my friend, and she didn't deserve my trust.

Even though she had been a bully when we were little, more recently we had actually had fun together. We had decorated her jewelry box together, we had played with the garden hose at her house once, and we had told each other about our crushes. But I decided, right then, that she was still the same mean, untrustworthy bully that she had always been.

Ruth called me back inside the classroom. I

came in and told her that Alana had backstabbed me. After our talk, I took my seat at my desk, and Ruth started reading aloud to the class.

As the hour droned by, I got more and more mad and embarrassed. Alana was no friend! She was a jerk who had backstabbed me when she had told me she wouldn't.

~*~

At the end of the day, I went out of the classroom and walked down the hall. I was passing my former classroom when my old teacher, Laura, beckoned me inside. She and Alana were sitting at a tiny table that had once fit me. I sat at the table with them.

Laura asked, "What happened?"

I said, "Alana backstabbed me! She told everyone about my crush on Rafaele and she also told him!"

Alana said, "I didn't tell Rafaele."

Laura talked some more with us, and it was concluded that Alana didn't tell Rafaele that I had a crush on him. Laura let us out of the classroom.

Later that week, I found out that Alana had been lying. She *did* tell Rafaele that I had a crush on him! On top of that, Justice and Courtney had stopped being friends; I had to sneak time with Justice so that Courtney wouldn't get mad. All of this social stuff was very difficult for me to understand and deal with!

During the school day, I played with Courtney. At the end of the day, when Courtney left, I felt free to play with Justice. I avoided Justice during the school day because I thought that Courtney was going to get mad at me for hanging out with Justice, and I wasn't confident enough to stand up for my friendship with her.

Courtney always left right at the end of the day. After school, Justice and I liked to play Musketeer Camp, where we were Musketeers. We called ourselves Hazel and Tori. I was Tori, and Justice was Hazel.

Justice and I would go to the garden and get sticks from the wood chips and call them swords. On good sword days, we found strong, long, swords with barely any splinters, or we found the good ones that we had used the day before. On bad sword days, we found weak, short, swords with tons of splinters.

We would have Musketeer camp next to the ball wall on the big side. We would set up camp and bring our backpacks there. We would picnic on food from snack time, and we would talk until the main daycare teacher, Linda, made everyone go over to the little side.

On the little side, Justice and I would set up camp in the grassy play area. One of the girls from the little side, Jazmine, sometimes played Musketeer Camp with us. My sister, Daisy, also played Musketeer Camp with us, and her Musketeer name was Claudia.

Justice seemed to be my only true friend at school at that point. Courtney was becoming less of a real friend, but it took a long time for me to figure that out.

One day, at the end of the day, I went to go play with Rafaele and his friends. They were in the field, playing a game where they were animals. I joined in with them.

They suggested that I be a cheetah because of my purple, cheetah-print tights, and I agreed with them.

We played until it was time for me to go. We planned to play the game again the next day, but we planned to dress like the animals we had been playing as. That meant that I had to dress like a cheetah.

The next day, I went to play with Rafaele's group at recess. Mom had helped me find the perfect cheetah outfit. It was an olive-green shirt with a pink butterfly on it, some shorts to go over my cheetah-print tights, and a pair of sneakers. Mom had a weird rule that I wasn't allowed to go in public without shorts or a skirt over my tights unless I was exercising.

I ran to the field where Rafaele and his friends were playing. They all wore clothes representing the animals they had played as the day before. We started playing the animal game.

I was having fun playing until I saw Courtney glaring at me. She was mad at me for playing with Rafaele and his friends.

Courtney left, and I continued playing with Rafaele and his friends. A few minutes later, I saw Courtney talking with Alana! I thought Courtney hated Alana! I ran to Courtney and Alana, and they turned their backs to me. They then went back to their talking.

Dad saw me trying to get their attention and told me that Courtney was already playing with Alana, as if I didn't know that already! There was a lot Dad didn't understand about what was happening.

I should've just abandoned my friendship with Courtney, but, instead, I let myself get pushed around by her. With autism, it was hard for me to understand people's intentions. I didn't recognize that Courtney wasn't really my friend, so I let myself be manipulated by her for a long time.

~*~

At the end of the day, Justice and I grabbed our backpacks and headed to the ball wall. I had an umbrella in my backpack, and I put it up as a tent.

Justice and I had fun at our camp. We ate butternut-squash soup that Dad had made. It had an amazing taste I could never forget.

Justice was a real friend. She disliked Courtney, but she never judged me for hanging out with her. Unlike my friendship with Courtney, my friendship with Justice was mutual.

It was time for me to go, and Mom and Dad took Daisy and me home. When we got home, we had dinner. Daisy and I got into our PJs, and then our family left the house to go back to Montessori.

Daisy and I were attending Movie Night at school. At Movie Night, Ruth and some other teachers would supervise the kids while they watched movies, played, and did arts and crafts. When we got there, Daisy went to play with her friends, and I saw Courtney.

Courtney gave me a Blenders in the Grass gift card. This was during the phase where she would grab gift cards off of shelves in stores and give them to other people, even though they had no money on them.

I thanked her and went to have a conversation with another kid. This made Courtney mad. She gave me a piece of paper that said, "You're excluding me and I don't like it."

I apologized and went to the table where kids were doing arts and crafts. I saw an empty egg carton in the recycling bin, and I took it out. I started crafting with it and drawing smiley faces on it with Sharpie.

Alana said that the egg carton was trash, but I didn't care. She then took it and threw it away, which made me furious. I got in an argument with her, and she just said that I dug the carton out of the trash, and it needed to go back.

I went to Ruth and told her that I wanted a desk reassignment. My desk was next to Alana's, and I didn't like sitting next to her. Ruth got a sticky note out and wrote a reminder to herself for the next day, "Move desks."

It was so kind of Ruth to move desks just to make me feel more comfortable. I felt very thankful for what she did.

Courtney and Alana started hanging out after winter break, and, soon, I no longer had Courtney as a friend.

It started when Courtney began hanging out with Alana on a Friday. Courtney promised that she would hang out with me on Monday and Tuesday, but on Monday, she ignored me completely and kept hanging out with Alana.

If I had been better at reading the social situation, I probably would've stopped hanging out with Courtney, but it was hard for me to understand that she was not really my friend.

When Courtney ignored me, I decided to play with Rafaele and his friends. Rafaele was still cute, but he and his friends did things that were absolutely disgusting to me. Twice, we had a picnic with lots of plants. They picked plants and put them in a huge pile in the center and ate them. I would spit the plants out on the side when the boys weren't paying attention.

On our second picnic, Alana and Courtney saw me chewing plants with the other kids, and I heard Courtney say, "That's disgusting." I left the picnic and followed Alana and Courtney around. They just ignored me.

When Tuesday rolled around, Alana was absent. It was Courtney's eighth birthday, and she got walkie-talkies as a gift! We played with them and giggled until the teacher saw that Ricardo wanted to play, but we weren't letting him. The teacher told

Courtney to put the walkie-talkies away.

We had fun that day, but, the next day, Alana came back. Courtney started hanging out with Alana and, again, I had nobody to play with until the end of the day when I played with Justice.

Courtney would judge me if I played with Justice, she would judge me if I played with Rafaele's group, and nobody else seemed interesting enough for me to play with.

I decided to hang out with Emma and her friend Hanna. Hanna and Emma were playing with their *Littlest Pet Shop* figurines (this was when *Littlest Pet Shop* was a big trend), but they wanted more alone time playing with their figurine collections, so they set a timer for when I could start playing with them. I played with them for a while that day, but then it got boring, and I can see now that they did not really want to play with me.

I ran to Courtney and Alana,
and they turned their backs to me.

Chapter 22

A Real Friend

I did not have any friends in my class. Then, a girl who had once visited Montessori for a day came back. The girl's name was Shannon.

When Shannon started school in Ruth's class, she came with two guinea pigs. Her guinea pigs, Mocha and Cookie, had this giant pen that the school let her keep in the yard.

Shannon was a little shy at first, but she and I started becoming friends. She was ten years old, a year older than me, and she had long red hair. She had a tooth that was a little crooked, which a couple of kids called a "vampire tooth," but I got used to it. I never saw it as abnormal, it was just part of her.

Shannon's name was easy for me to remember because there was a fairy in the *Rainbow Magic* books who was named Shannon.

Shannon and I liked playing with her guinea pigs. She let kids hold them, and, once, Cookie peed on a boy in our class. Cookie was the skittish one. Mocha was the one who allowed everyone to hold her.

Shannon and I sometimes talked at recess. We found that we had some things in common. We both liked reading the *Whatever After* series, which is about a girl named Abby, and her brother, Jonah, who own a magic mirror and change the endings of fairy tales.

When Shannon played at my house one time, we played a game where she was a princess, and I was a mermaid named Chloe. In our game, the princess was captured by an evil person, and she needed to get out so she could marry the man she loved, Hudson! I was a mermaid who was captured and needed to get back to the sea!

In our game, we got free, and then Hudson turned psycho. Now the princess needed to escape from Hudson (it was all very weird and nonsensical)!

We also played this same game at her house, but at her house, we had costumes! I got to wear a mermaid costume, and she wore a princess costume!

Another time, we went to go see a movie together. We went to a movie theater in Oxnard and watched *Home*. It was a funny movie about aliens called Boovs taking over the Earth. Unlike most of the other kids I knew at school, Shannon was a real friend, who I will never forget, but she soon left Montessori school.

Chapter 23

Fake Friends

After Shannon left Montessori, I was back to hanging out with Courtney. We usually invited Alana to hang out with us. Some days it was actually quite nice, but mostly it was peer pressure.

Once, Courtney tried to get me to buy her a tiny notebook with my money, and I just cried and said no. Another time, Alana tried to buy a book that she wanted, from the used book market at school, by telling the teacher that she found a half-dollar on the ground (it was mine!). This was a ridiculous lie that she told. She should have just gone up with my money and bought the book she wanted and not have tried to make up some weird backstory. Her lies were normally pretty good, but this one was just plain stupid. Later, Courtney and I stopped hanging out with Alana because Courtney thought she was a tattletale.

When Courtney and I played together, one of our favorite things to do was tease Simon, my "ex-boyfriend," and play pranks on him. Courtney liked picking on him, and I went along with it because my "friend" didn't like him. We had a lot of ideas for playing mean pranks on him, but our worst prank was to put bees in his lunchbox.

One night, my mom asked me if there was anything I had ever been afraid to tell her. I started sobbing. I told Mom that Courtney and I were putting bees in Simon's lunchbox and playing other pranks. My mom was horrified that I had been a part of mean behavior like that, and that I had been keeping it inside for so long when I felt bad about it!

Mom hugged me and told me that all the behavior was mean, but that putting bees in someone's lunchbox was also very dangerous because what if Simon was allergic?

This conversation, along with hearing some of my social problems, was what made my parents decide that I might need a school with more supervision and better social support.

One day, at lunch, Courtney suggested that we put more bees in Simon's lunchbox.

I said, "No, because Simon could be allergic and he could go to the hospital!"

Courtney could tell that I had told an adult about our prank, so she said, "You shouldn't have told!"

I ran to the bathroom and cried. If I didn't have autism, I might have told Courtney, "It's not right to hurt somebody just because we don't like him. How would you feel if you went to the hospital because some obnoxious kids put bees in your lunchbox?"

I would've stopped being friends with Courtney. I would've been able to tell from the start that she was a fake friend. Sure, she and I had been good friends when we were little, but when something doesn't feel right in a friendship, it's time to find new friends. It's time to get rid of the fake friendship and move on. Moving on can be difficult, especially when you have autism.

Another time Courtney and Alana manipulated me was at a festival that my school did every year. This event had cool games, rides, and fun activities.

On this day, I purchased forty tickets with the twenty dollars Mom had given me. When I saw Courtney and Alana, I told them I had forty tickets. Courtney asked me for six tickets for an activity. Alana asked me for ten tickets so that she could go on the pony ride. In total, I gave away sixteen tickets. I then went off to do my own activities and, at the end of the day, Mom and I went home.

In the car, I told Mom that I had given away sixteen of my tickets. Mom was annoyed at me for this. She told me that she had not paid for tickets for me to just give them away. In the end, this mistake cost me eight dollars! I had to repay Mom for all the tickets I had given away. She even made me do the math to figure out how much money I had to pay her back.

If I didn't have autism, I might've understood that Courtney and Alana were taking advantage of me. I might've said to them, "No, I'm not going to give you guys that many tickets! Get your own!"

But instead, I lost eight dollars. I could've spent eight dollars on something else I wanted. I didn't have to spend money on fake friends.

Chapter 24

The Change I Needed

A few weeks after my school year ended, Mom and Dad decided that I was old enough for a phone. They decided that I was getting more mature and was ready for this responsibility.

One day, Mom and Dad took me to Verizon to get my new phone. They set out to get me the coolest iPhone, which was the iPhone Six Plus. It was the newest one at the time. They placed an order for my phone and, soon, my phone was going to be delivered to our house.

As Mom and Dad worked out the details at Verizon, I checked out the iPhone Six Plus that was on display. I played a Sonic the Hedgehog game that I planned to get on my future phone.

Getting a phone was a way to help me connect with friends. I could keep in touch and plan hangouts, which was important for me. A phone would also allow me to have more freedom and independence. I could go around town with friends and just call Mom or Dad if I had any problems or needed anything.

Another change that occured that summer was that I made a real best friend. While I had had a few school friends over the years, I had only had one really good friend for most of my childhood. This really good friend was a girl named Gianna, who I had known since I was five.

Gianna and I did a social skills group with CIO when I was younger. We liked to be together, but we never got to hang out too much because we lived in separate cities and went to separate schools. She was a real friend, and we had always liked and accepted each other. Like me, Gianna had social skills challenges, and we were able to connect because we didn't expect each other to be any different than the way we were. Gianna and I are still friends to this day.

The summer I was nine, the girl who became my best friend was Kali. We met at the learning camp Mom had every summer at her clinic.

I became best friends with Kali because of a yogurt cup. It sounds silly but, one day, I didn't have a snack packed. Kali knew I was snackless, so she offered me some of hers.

For her snack, she had a whole peach and a blueberry yogurt cup; I chose the yogurt cup when she offered.

The yogurt cup was just the start of our friendship. In a few weeks, Kali became my closest friend. We liked to play Minecraft together. We also played with American Girl dolls together, went to the mall, went to the county fair, went swimming at each other's houses, and had sleepovers. It was great to have a real best friend who I could spend lots of time with!

Before Kali, the close friends that I had were mostly either younger than me, or they had social challenges that were similar to mine. When I was hanging out with Courtney and Alana, I called them my friends, but I felt little value in myself, and I didn't like who I was with them. They were not real friends.

Kali was my age, and she didn't have any social challenges, but she accepted me for me. I felt more value in myself knowing that she was my friend, and this was a change I needed.

The change that benefited me the most was going to a different school. Montessori was a great place for me to learn when I was young, but, as I got older, things got more complicated. I wasn't able to handle some of the social situations that I faced on my own.

The summer I was nine, Mom asked me if I wanted to go to the new school she was starting. To tell the truth, I had never really thought about it until Mom asked me. It is a very small school specifically for kids who are having trouble learning in other settings.

I told Mom that I wanted to go to her school, and I became a student of the Lighthouse School, where I have been for the past three school years.

At this new school, I made new friends. At first there were just four of us, and we were all in fourth or fifth grade. A girl named Ruby, a boy named Jonas, and a girl named Sofia went to school with me.

I knew Sofia from when I was younger, and she would come to Mom's learning clinic for help with reading. She had a lisp and wore glasses and was really funny. When we were little, we would sometimes play together in the playroom at the office.

I also knew Ruby from when I was younger. We knew each other from Mom's summer learning camp. She was a wild, funny girl who often wore fancy clothes and costumes.

That first year, with only four students, was three whole years ago! Now, I am in middle school and I go to the Lighthouse School with my amazing friends; there are way more kids now than there were at first. My friends are all very understanding of my challenges, and they accept me for who I am because they, too, have different learning and social challenges that they're working to overcome.

I get taught five days a week by my amazing teachers. At Lighthouse, the kids know the teachers better than they would know their teachers at a typical school. We have actual conversations with our teachers, and they ask for student feedback on important issues and decisions about school activities.

At school, I'm continuing to work on my social

skills. In our *Social Thinking* classes, we learn about things that are necessary for socializing as you get older, like flirting (basically showing people that you are interested in them) and social faking (pretending you are interested in other people's conversation even when they aren't that interesting). I work on staying on topic (a lot of the students work on this), and I work on being a more flexible thinker, which means letting some things go for the moment.

I'm now able to fight a fair fight with people my age; I don't need an adult to step in. I can develop my own opinions without other people's input. I can tell a real friend from a fake friend, and I understand other people's perspectives and can empathize.

I've become stronger academically. I love to read, and I'm great at writing and math. I've learned about human psychology and behavior, and I'm passionate about social justice; I create YouTube videos with my friends about important issues such as gun violence and understanding learning challenges. I perform in musicals with a local theater company.

If I didn't change schools and get the help I

needed, I wouldn't be writing a memoir, I probably wouldn't be able to do many of the things I'm now good at, and I wouldn't be the person I am today.

Courtney and Alana shaped me. They were mean at times, but they are part of my past. They're the reason I can distinguish fake friends from real friends. When I see them now, I can see that they've grown up a lot too, and I don't hold a grudge as I did for so long.

My current friends have shaped me. They are really genuine, and they are part of my life now. They've helped me become a better person, and they've helped me open up. When I was younger, I would only have playdates a few times a year, but now I hang out with my friends too many times to count!

My teachers have shaped me. They've helped me learn, and they've helped me develop into the student that I am. I feel very lucky to have the education that I have today. I have my loving and accepting friends by my side, and I have my supportive family with me as I continue to learn and grow!

To Be Continued

There is so much more I'd like to write, and I have so much more ahead of me in my life. I wrote this memoir because I want to show people how I see the world, as a person with autism. I want to explain how my life has been different from many other people's lives, and how certain thoughts and ideas came into my mind that other people did not understand. I want to share why I did things that seemed strange to others.

I wanted to express myself by writing a book about my life, instead of merely talking about my memories with my family, because I want to put an end to the idea that autism is a disease that needs a "cure." I want to put an end to autism being a taboo subject.

I hope that, when you close this book, you have more understanding about what life can be like for a person with autism and the challenges that some people face.

ACKNOWLEDGEMENTS
By Gloria and Jon Ellis

There are so many people to thank who helped make this project become a reality for Micaela.

We would like to thank Mickie's teacher, Jamaica Thompson, for supporting her in this project and providing invaluable feedback throughout the process.

Thank you to Vivian Sudhalter, who provided her editing expertise, Holly Roberts, who volunteered her time to create and capture a beautiful cover photograph, and Alex Mooney, who designed a gorgeous book cover for Mickie.

Many thanks to our very supportive family- most especially, to Pop-Pop, Grandma Ethel, and Aunt Becca, who did not make any major appearances in this memoir, but whose love, support, and respect for Mickie, through all the stages of her learning, have been a constant source of comfort and reassurance.

We so appreciate the many educators at the Montessori School who always gave their time, energy, respect, and affection to our daughter!

There have been many therapists who were instrumental in helping Mickie develop her skills, including the staff of the Assistance League School in Oxnard, Occupational Therapist Michaela Gordon, the staff of Passport to Adaptive Living (formerly CIO) in Ventura, the staff of Communication Matters in Newbury Park, Speech and Language Pathologist Cheryl Fletcher, the staff of Tri-Counties Regional Center, Special Education Advocate Lori Boehm, and numerous other individuals and teams who have supplied their time and expertise in support of Micaela's growth.

We are incredibly grateful to all of the kids, at Montessori School and at the Lighthouse School, who have taught Mickie what it means to have a friend, and to be a friend, over the years.